READY TO

READY TO READ

by
Ruth Brancard
and
Jeanne Hind

Oxford University Press

Oxford University Press

198 Madison Avenue
New York, NY 10016 USA

Great Clarendon Street
Oxford OX2 6DP England

Oxford   New York
Athens Auckland Bangkok Bogota Bombay Buenos Aires
Calcutta Cape Town Dar es Salaam Delhi Florence Hong Kong
Istanbul Karachi Kuala Lumpur Madras Madrid Melbourne
Mexico City Nairobi Paris Singapore Taipei Tokyo Toronto Warsaw

and associated companies in
Berlin Ibadan

OXFORD is a trademark of Oxford University Press.

Library of Congress Cataloging-in-Publication Data

Brancard, Ruth.
     Ready to read : a beginning ESL reading text / by Ruth Brancard
and Jeanne Hind.
          p.   cm.
     ISBN 0-19-434368-5
     1. English language—Textbooks for foreign speakers.
2. Readers—1950—   I. Hind, Jeanne.   II. Title.
PE1128.B659   1989
428.6′4—dc19   89-30072
                                                    CIP

Associate Editor: Mary Lynne Nielsen
Designer: Mark Kellogg
Art Researcher: Paula Radding
Production Coordinator: Ellen Foos

Cover design by Mark Kellogg.

Cover photographs by George Bellerose/Stock, Boston; Tom Carter, courtesy of the *Peoria Journal Star*; the *Denver Post*; Denver Public Library, Western History Department; and River Cruises.

Illustrations by Frederick Porter, Larry Raymond, Carolyn Vibbert, and Clare Wood.

Graphics by Alan Barnett, Maj-Britt Hagsted, Terry Helms, and April Okano.
Maps by Graphic Chart and Map Co.

Since this page cannot legibly accommodate all the copyright notices, page v constitutes an extension of the copyright page.

Photographs by Ron Alexander/Stock, Boston; Mark Antman/The Image Works; George Bellerose/Stock, Boston; Ruth Brancard; Tom Carter, courtesy of the *Peoria Journal Star*; Elizabeth Crews/Stock, Boston; Mimi Forsyth; Hazel Hankin/Stock, Boston; Joe Hayes; Jeanne Hind; Larry J. Hunt and Jerry Jacka, courtesy of Artists of Indian America; John Running/Stock, Boston; Susan Woog Wagner/Photo Researchers; and Janet Zehr.

Other photographs and prints courtesy of Antman Archives/The Image Works; Artists of Indian America; The Bettmann Archive; The Carr Collection; the *Denver Post*; The Denver Public Library, Western History Department; and River Cruises.

The chart on page 147 is from the "Highest mountains in the world" table in *Encyclopaedia Britannica*, 15th edition (1989), 8:375. Reprinted by permission.

Printing (last digit): 10 9 8 7 6

Printed in China

Contents

Acknowledgments

We could not have written this book without the help of some very special people. First, we would like to thank Hue Truong, Daddy Bruce, Susan and Cecil Graber, Joe Hayes, and Dennis Trone for giving their time. We would also like to thank Carolyn Hind, Jeanne's great-aunt, whose book about her great-aunt is the basis for our chapter about Julia Brier. Special thanks need to go to Elizabeth Carr, Tom and Mike Carr, and Bonnie Jo Hunt for not only the interviews but also their assistance with photographs and their enthusiastic involvement in the project. Without the work of Janet Zehr our book would be picture poor. Thanks to her for the interview with Dennis Trone, the pictures, and her time and energy.

We would also like to recognize Jan Fitzgerald for her assistance and friendship, Steve Cox of the *Denver Post* for his quick responses to our requests for pictures, and Lin Denham and Connie Shoemaker for their interview suggestions. Finally, we would like to thank all of our beginning reading students who used this material during its various stages of development and provided the motivation for taking on this project. Their feedback on the chapters and exercises was invaluable.

This book is dedicated to Connie Shoemaker, Pambos Polycarpou, and all our colleagues at Spring International Language Center. Without the computers, reams of paper, and the copier, the task of doing the manuscript would have been overwhelming. More importantly, they allowed us time from our work schedules to complete the book and gave us constant encouragement.

Notes to the Teacher

The following assumptions about the nature of the reading process are central to the approach followed in *Ready to Read*:

1. Students' background knowledge about the subject of a reading plays a key role in their ability to understand the reading. Current reading research supports the theory that readers understand what they read by relating it to what they already know, and, where necessary, modifying what they know to accommodate the new information that they have gained from the written page.

2. Adult learners of English need material appropriate for adults. The fact that learners have an elementary knowledge of English does not mean they are incapable of thinking about more complex ideas. In fact, reading material about more complex ideas is more likely to engage them and may well improve comprehension.

3. Reading comprehension improves when readers have a purpose for reading; in other words, when they are reading to answer questions. Readers understand when they focus on getting information rather than on decoding words.

4. A great deal of reading practice is necessary to improve reading comprehension and fluency.

5. A reader can comprehend grammatical structures that he cannot analyze or produce. The early chapters make very limited use of the past tense and complex sentences, but these structures appear more frequently in later chapters.

Ready to Read is designed as a first reading text for adult and young adult learners of English as a second language. There are nine chapters and 20 supplemental readings. Each chapter has the following sections:

GETTING IDEAS
BUILDING IDEAS
GETTING READY TO READ
LET'S GO
AFTER READING
READING HELPERS

The LET'S GO section is followed by the reading. The 20 supplemental readings referred to at the end of each chapter are found in the back of the book in the first appendix.

GETTING IDEAS

The first page of each chapter has a photograph with questions under it. The purpose of the photograph is to start discussion on a subject. The questions serve as guides to the discussion, not absolute directives. The discussion allows students to recall what they know about a subject and to share their knowledge with the teacher and the rest of the class. It's a good idea for the teacher to write words on the board as they come up in the discussion. This part of the lesson usually takes about 15–20 minutes.

BUILDING IDEAS

This part of the chapter is similar in purpose to GETTING IDEAS, but the discussion becomes more exact in order to elicit more specific vocabulary from students and to show connections between ideas. Using the blackboard, the teacher builds a network of ideas around a central idea. The teacher writes the students' ideas on the board in a way that shows logical connections between the ideas. (See the example in Chapter 1.) It is important that this be a class activity rather than homework because students can learn from each other. The teacher can also contribute ideas. For the first few lessons, students should be allowed time to copy notes from the blackboard into the space provided in the book. However, in a short time, students will automatically write the networks in their books. This activity usually takes 20–25 minutes of class time.

In addition to the introduction of vocabulary, these first two parts of each lesson provide a framework of ideas that the reader then uses to interact with the reading.

GETTING READY TO READ

This section of each chapter provides a series of exercises, usually requiring group interaction, that will further develop students' background and language knowledge in ways that will help them to understand the reading. The first exercises are usually word focused—for example, recognizing synonyms and antonyms—or related to graphic clues like pictures, capital letters, maps, and graphs.

The last exercise in this section is usually "getting information from sentences." This exercise is a list of sentences derived from the reading. The teacher should ask the question, "What information can you get from this sentence?" rather than "What's the subject of the sentence?" or "What's the verb?" Questioning about information encourages students to pull ideas from sentences. This exercise helps students to recognize where facts are within a sentence and allows some careful sentence study without going through a reading word by word. Sentences have been selected from the reading for various reasons, such as key concepts, important or difficult grammatical structures, or new vocabulary that they contain. In this way, vocabulary can be discussed with some context rather than in a list. When students encounter a familiar sentence in the reading, the sentence is like a safe home.

Some parts of GETTING READY TO READ can be assigned as homework. Approximately one class period will be required for this part of the chapter.

LET'S GO

Purpose-setting questions and the reading are included in this section. Students are encouraged to preview the title of the reading, the pictures, and the captions and to say what they think the reading will be about. Questions are provided before each reading in the first chapters. These questions give students a purpose for reading. They help to get students actively involved in understanding meaning as they read. In later chapters, students are guided to generate their own questions before reading.

Now that all of the groundwork has been laid, students should be able to read the text with minimal help from the teacher. Students should read silently, asking for help when they cannot understand. When asked for help, the teacher can guide students to find meaning from context and background knowledge. Teachers should encourage students to use the text to understand meaning whenever possible and that dictionaries are to be used only after context has failed them. The amount of time required for the reading varies with the student and the length of the reading. Some of the reading can be done in class and some can be done as homework.

AFTER READING

The first exercise and sometimes the second in this section are comprehension checks. Students will finish the reading at different times and can complete these comprehension exercises on their own. The teacher can help students with errors by pointing out the portion of the text that they need to reread in order to correct their mistakes in understanding. Mistakes in the comprehension exercises should serve as guides to the teacher about which parts of the text need to be explained to an individual student or which parts should be discussed by the whole group. The comprehension exercises are not intended to be used as tests.

All of the chapters contain an exercise that requires students to organize information from the reading and represent it in a way that aids memory. The purpose of this exercise is to provide students with models for ways of extracting important ideas from a reading and framing them in a way that helps them to retain information. These exercises provide alternatives to the question, ''What's the main idea of this paragraph?'' While we do introduce the concept of the main idea, we think that these alternatives offer a more workable framework for finding important information. These exercises are, in fact, first steps toward summary writing.

Word-study exercises are also provided in this section. These can be done individually or as a group. These exercises include work with affixes, parts of speech, words with multiple meanings, and past tense forms. At least one class period should be spent on this section and any discussions that result from it.

READING HELPERS

The purpose of this section is to summarize and explain the reasons for the reading strategies that are taught in the chapters. The strategy explained in a chapter may be one that has been emphasized in that chapter. Often it is a strategy that becomes particularly important in the following chapter. The teacher should read this section of each lesson with the students to help them understand the method and purpose of the strategies. This usually takes no more than 10–15 minutes.

SUPPLEMENTAL READINGS

At the end of each chapter under the heading MORE READING is list of supplemental readings that are related to that chapter. However, the teacher may want to choose other readings to fit individual student needs and interests. A teacher might also decide to have students read a supplemental reading before doing the chapter in order to better prepare them for the chapter. Because most of the readings can be read independently, they can be assigned to students who finish early and need more work to do in class, or they can be given as homework assignments. With the help of the supplemental readings the teacher can increase the amount of reading that students do. As with the readings in each chapter, the amount of time required varies with the students and the length of the particular supplemental reading they are using.

The readings in each chapter, with two exceptions, are based on interviews with Americans. The exceptions include a reading based on an interview with a Vietnamese immigrant and an adaptation of a diary of a pioneer woman. Adult students are attracted to this nonfiction aspect of the reading content.

The readings in this text are longer than most reading texts for beginning readers. We believe this aids comprehension and fluency. Reading comprehension depends on the reader's active participation in the reading process. The reader reviews his existing knowledge about the subject of the reading, formulates questions about the reading, predicts the information in the reading, and revises his ideas about the subject as he takes in more information from the written page. Short readings do not allow the reader to get this process going.

Another feature of the book that might cause initial concern is the use of some specialized vocabulary. Teachers may react negatively to this aspect of the book with the argument that students will never need to know these words. The reason for the inclusion of this vocabulary is not to have students memorize these words, but rather to make it possible to write about subjects likely to interest students. Chapter 4 is about a river steamboat and includes some of the most specialized vocabulary in the book. It is not the purpose of the reading that students remember the words *paddlewheel* and *deckhand*. In field tests of this book, students have had no problem with these words because they were interested in the subject. The chapter about the steamboat has consistently been one of the most popular with students. Of course, students should not be tested on their ability to recall these words. However, these words are necessary to explain the subject.

An emphasis on the importance of prereading activities is a key feature of *Ready to Read*. While these activities take a fair amount of class time, we feel they are indispensable. Students who have completed the prereading activities can usually understand the reading with a minimum of teacher assistance.

The supplemental readings at the end of the book are another unique feature of this text. These readings accommodate individual learning rates. Despite the best efforts at testing and placement, students enter beginning language classes with varied proficiency levels. Their language backgrounds and a variety of other factors affect each student's rate of progress. The supplemental readings provide additional reading for the faster student. A slower student can get more reading practice from the easier supplemental readings while other class members progress to a more difficult reading.

The supplemental readings are related in subject matter to the main readings, but they appear at the end of the book. Their placement makes the book more flexible. Advanced students can have additional work, while slower students won't feel that they have "skipped" readings or failed to complete part of the chapter.

In summary, we would like to note that we have used these lessons in various stages of their development in our beginning-level reading classes for two years. This approach to reading works well for us and our students. We are seeing better readers as a result of the teaching strategies used with this text. We hope it works well for you, too.

Ruth Brancard
Jeanne Hind
May 1988

READY TO READ

Chapter 1
Learning English

GETTING IDEAS

1. What can you see in this picture?
2. What are the students doing?
3. Where are the students from?
4. Why are they here?

BUILDING IDEAS

An **idea** is a picture in the mind. When you read, you picture a story.

Read this sentence: *My mother is cooking dinner in the kitchen.* What picture is in your mind after you read this? What pictures do your classmates have? Discuss this in class.

Each person has a different picture. Each person sees a different person and smells a different food. When you read, you bring your ideas and experiences with you. **You** and your ideas are an important part of the reading.

In this section, we are going to build ideas for the reading in this chapter. We are also going to build vocabulary, or words, for the reading. For example, look at this word: English. What do you think of when you read this word? What ideas do you have? We can draw ideas about this word like this:

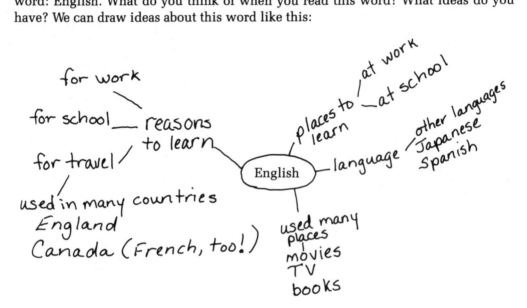

Do you see how many ideas a person can have from one word? Can you add ideas to this picture?

We are going to build ideas about learning English. What ideas do you have for the following phrases?

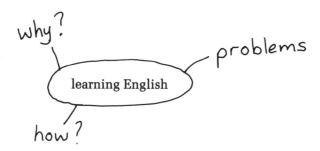

GETTING READY TO READ

Exercise 1

Take a walk around your classroom and the building you are in. Write down some of the English words you see. Bring your list back to class. Talk about the words with your class. What words are important to you?

My List of Words

Exercise 2

The alphabet is important. We use it in many ways. For example, the dictionary uses the alphabet. Words are arranged in **alphabetical order** in the dictionary.

This means that the words are in the same order as the letters of the alphabet. Do you understand **order**?

Ask each student in your class the month and day of his or her birthday. Stand in a line in the order of your birthdays. Whose birthday comes first in a year beginning January 1? Whose birthday is next? The line is in the **order** of birthdays.

Ask each student in your class his or her first name. What is the first letter? Stand in a line using the order of the alphabet. Whose name begins with an **A**? The line is in **alphabetical order.**

Rewrite these words in alphabetical order:

book	alphabet	class	student	year
home	teacher	work	letter	school
name	dictionary	boat	pencil	word

_____ _____ _____

_____ _____ _____

_____ _____ _____

_____ _____ _____

_____ _____ _____

Exercise 3

Sentences give us information. What information does each sentence give us?

For example, look at this sentence: *Hue Truong is a student.* This sentence tells us the person's name. It also tells us what Hue does.

What information do these sentences give us? Read each sentence and talk about the information in it with your class.

1. Hue Truong is 13 years old.
2. Hue's father wants the family to leave Vietnam.
3. Hue wants to help her mother and father, but she wants to go to school, too.
4. Hue is nervous because she doesn't know English.
5. Her class has many foreign students. They are from Vietnam, Switzerland, Japan, Mexico, Hong Kong, and Taiwan.
6. Spelling is difficult in English.

LET'S GO

Getting ready to read is very important. You can do this by looking at the title of a reading and the pictures. What do you think the reading is about? You can get ready to read by asking yourself questions. As you read, think about the answers to these questions:

1. Who is Hue Truong?
2. Why does she leave Vietnam?
3. How does she get to Hong Kong?
4. When does she come to the United States?
5. What does she learn in school?
6. What is Hue doing now?

———————————— Are you ready to read? ————————————

Hue Truong: Working Hard for What She Wants

It is 1981. Hue Truong is 13 years old. She is living in Vietnam. Life is hard for Hue's family in 1981. Her father and mother have six children. Hue is the oldest child. She has four sisters and one brother. Hue does not go to school. She stays at home. She cooks and takes care of her sisters and brother. Her mother and father work hard. She wants to help her mother and father, but she wants to go to school, too.

Hue's father wants the family to leave Vietnam. He has a boat. Hue's family gets on the boat. An aunt and uncle come, too. Other people get on the boat. There are 27 people on the small boat. They leave Vietnam at night. No one sees them. No one stops them. They are on the boat for seven days. They travel more than 600 miles (965 kilometers). Then they arrive in Hong Kong. They are safe.

They live in Hong Kong for one year. Hue wants to learn English, but it is difficult. She wants to go to school. She wants a new home. But she can't have these things. Hue and her family cannot stay in Hong Kong. An aunt and uncle live in the United States of America. Hue and her family want to go to the USA, too. Hue wants to go to school and learn English in the United States.

It is 1982. The Truong family leaves Hong Kong. They come to the United States. Hue is 14 years old now. She can't speak English. She can say, "Hi." That is all. She is nervous because she doesn't know English. Everything is new.

She goes to a junior high school. Her class has many foreign students. They are from Vietnam, Switzerland, Japan, Mexico, Hong Kong, and Taiwan. She wants to make friends with them. All of the students are learning English. Hue wants to learn English, too. They study English three hours a day. The students are friendly. The teacher is nice. Everyone helps Hue. Soon she is not nervous. She is happy because she can go to school.

Hue likes to meet other students at her school.

First, Hue learns the English alphabet. She learns the names of the letters. She learns the sounds of the letters, too. It is not easy. One letter can have different sounds, and one sound can have different spellings. Spelling is difficult in English. It is not easy, but Hue learns the alphabet. The alphabet is important for Hue. She uses the alphabet to read English. She uses the alphabet to find words in the dictionary. She works hard because she wants to be a good student.

Hue's father buys a dictionary. It is for the family. It is very big. Hue cannot take it to school. Every day she hears new words at school. Every day she comes home and looks up new words in the dictionary. The dictionary has two languages in it. It has Vietnamese and English in it. It is a bilingual dictionary, a dictionary with two languages.

Hue studies every day. She learns the alphabet. Now she can use the telephone book. She also learns to count in English. The numbers are important. Now she can say her telephone number. Then she learns the names of the days and months. Soon she is speaking English with her new friends at the school.

Hue helps a student in the computer lab.

It is 1988. Hue is twenty years old. Now she is studying at a college. She works at the college, too. She works in the computer lab. She helps American and foreign students with the computers. Her English is very good. She is a good student. In the future, Hue wants to graduate from college. She wants to get a good job. She plans to marry.

Hue can speak English well now. Hue says this to other foreign students, "Learning English is difficult, but you can learn it. Study hard. Soon you will understand more and more. Soon you will speak, read, and write English well."

AFTER READING

Write T if the sentence is true (right) and F if the sentence is false (wrong). If the sentence is false, rewrite it with the correct information.

_____ 1. Hue is from Vietnam.

_____

_____ 2. Hue goes to school in Vietnam.

_____

_____ 3. Hue and her family go to Malaysia in a boat.

_____

_____ 4. The alphabet and dictionary are important for students.

_____

_____ 5. Hue's class has many American students in it.

_____

You can answer certain questions with *yes* or *no*. These questions usually begin with the *be* verb (am, is, are) or the words *do* or *does*.

Answer these questions with *yes* or *no*.

1. Is Hue living in the United States in 1981?

_____

2. Does her father want to leave Vietnam?

_____

3. Are the people in her class foreign students?

_____

4. Does Hue study five hours of English a day at school?

_____

5. Is Hue studying in high school in 1988?

_____

Exercise 3

There are also questions that begin with the words *who, what, where, when, why,* and *how.* The answer to these questions cannot be *yes* or *no.* The answer needs more information. For example: *What country are you from? I'm from the United States.*
    Answer these questions with the correct information.

1. Who is Hue Truong?

_____

2. Why does she leave Vietnam?

_____

3. How does she get to Hong Kong?

_____

4. When does she come to the United States?

_____

5. What is Hue doing now?

_____

Exercise 4

After we read, we want to remember the main ideas of the reading. In this story, Hue wants to do many things. You can remember some facts of the story by recalling the places, the years, and the things Hue wants. Look back at the reading. What does Hue want to do during each of the times on the chart? Complete the chart on the next page.

	Hue wants to . . .	Can she do this? What do you think?
In Vietnam (1981)		
In Hong Kong (1981–1982)		
In the USA (1982–1988)		

Exercise 5

Complete each sentence with the correct word from the list.

bilingual	foreign	books	alphabetical	important

1. Dictionaries are very important _____.

2. Students from other countries are _____ students.

3. The dictionary is arranged in _____ order.

4. The alphabet is _____. We use it a lot.

5. A dictionary with two languages in it is a _____ dictionary.

Exercise 6—Word Study

There are different kinds of words. Some words are **nouns.** A noun is the name for a person, place, or thing. Here are some examples of nouns: *book, pen, school, desk,* and *door.* Can you think of some more examples?

_____   _____   _____   _____   _____

Look back at the reading and write down ten nouns.

_____	_____	_____	_____	_____
_____	_____	_____	_____	_____

Another kind of word is a **verb.** Verbs are very important. Verbs tell the action of the sentence. Here are some examples of verbs: *run, speak, cook,* and *study.* Can you think of some more examples?

_____	_____	_____	_____	_____

Look back at the reading and write down ten verbs.

_____	_____	_____	_____	_____
_____	_____	_____	_____	_____

READING HELPERS

```
A  B  C  D  E  F  G  H  I  J  K  L  M  N  O  P  Q  R  S  T  U  V  W  X  Y  Z
a  b  c  d  e  f  g  h  i  j  k  l  m  n  o  p  q  r  s  t  u  v  w  x  y  z
```

Here is the English alphabet. The letters are **type.** A typewriter writes the letters. First you see capital letters. Then you see small letters.

A B C D E F G H I J K L M N O P Q R S T U V W X Y Z
a b c d e f g h i j k l m n o p q r s t u v w x y z

Here is the English alphabet again. The letters are **print** letters. A person writes the letters, not a typewriter. The capital letters and small letters are different. The letters in a word are not connected.

A B C D E F G H I J K L M N O P Q R S T U V W X Y Z
a b c d e f g h i j k l m n o p q r s t u v w x y z

A person writes these letters, too. They are different from print. We call this **script** or **cursive**. The letters in a word are connected.

We use type in books. Teachers use type for tests. People use print for application and registration forms. Teachers sometimes use print on the blackboard. People use cursive for compositions, letters to friends, and signing their names. Teachers sometimes use cursive on the blackboard. You must learn these kinds of writing.

Here is a name in print: *Hue Truong*

Here is a signature: *Hue Truong*

Here is a form. Can you fill it out?

Print your family name and given name.
Leave a blank box between names.

1. Name

2. Mailing Address

Print your street address on one line.
Print your city, state, and zip code on the other lines.

Sign Here: _____   _____
                      Signature   Date

MORE READING

Supplemental Reading 1—"What's Your Name?"
Supplemental Reading 2—"Maria Starts School"

Chapter 2
Enjoying a Job

GETTING IDEAS

1. What can you see in this picture?
2. What is this person's job?
3. Where is this person working?
4. Is this an important job?

BUILDING IDEAS

We are going to build ideas about jobs at a school. Think about the people at your school. Who are they? What does each person do? How are they important to the school? Then think about the things a secretary must do at an office. What are the duties of a secretary?

people at school

duties of a secretary

GETTING READY TO READ

Exercise 1

Circle the two words that are specific examples of the general word on the left.

1. **job**	doctor	teacher	school
2. **country**	Colorado	Japan	Mexico
3. **language**	Spanish	USA	French
4. **class**	grammar	writing	teacher
5. **number**	job	one	nine

6.	**meal**	lunch	water	dinner
7.	**family**	mother	son	car
8.	**money**	dollar	dime	bank
9.	**food**	apple	pencil	hamburger
10.	**sport**	tennis	football	eating

Exercise 2

You can understand a sentence when you do not have all the words in the sentence. You can guess the missing word from the rest of the information in the sentence. Many times you can understand the sentence without the word. Look at this sentence: *It is raining. I don't want to get wet. I need an* _____. You can guess that the missing word is *umbrella.*

Maybe you do not know the word *umbrella,* but you have a picture in your mind. You do not need the word *umbrella* to understand the sentence. When you read, you sometimes guess the next word. You use information in the sentence to understand the word.

Look at these sentences. Think of a word that can complete each sentence. You can do this when you use the rest of the information in the sentence.

1. At the school, many students from foreign _____ learn English.

2. She eats _____ from 1:00 to 1:30 P.M. every day.

3. A secretary answers the _____ and types _____.

4. Sometimes she takes the students to the _____ when they feel sick.

5. It is important to know your address and telephone _____.

6. The classes are grammar, reading, and _____.

Exercise 3

Sentences give us information. Read each sentence and talk about the information in it with your class.

1. Elizabeth Carr is a secretary.
2. The school is an English language school.
3. She works every day, but she doesn't work all day.
4. She leaves work at 4:00 P.M. every day.
5. She orders supplies. For example, she orders pencils, pens, and notebooks.
6. Sometimes a caller wants to learn English at the school.
7. Elizabeth helps the students find their classes.

LET'S GO

Now you are going to read. Look at the title of the reading, and look at the pictures and captions. What do you think the reading is about? As you read, think about the answers to these questions:

1. Who is Elizabeth?
2. What is her job?
3. What are her duties?
4. How many hours a day does she work?
5. What are some questions people ask Elizabeth?
6. Why do the students like Elizabeth?
7. Why does Elizabeth work?

——————————— Are you ready to read? ———————————

Elizabeth Carr: A Very Important Person

Elizabeth Carr works in an office. She is a secretary at a language school. It is an English language school. There are many teachers at the school. They teach English to students from foreign countries. Elizabeth is a very important person to everyone at the office. She does many things, and she helps many people.

The students at the school come from many countries. They speak many different languages. Elizabeth likes meeting the students. She likes learning about their countries. She likes helping them. Elizabeth is a very important person to the students.

Elizabeth works every day, but she doesn't work all day. Many people come to work at 8:30 A.M. and leave work at 5:00 P.M. These people are full-time workers. Elizabeth doesn't work full-time. She comes to work at 11:30 A.M. and leaves work at 4:00 P.M. She eats lunch from 1:00 to 1:30 P.M. Elizabeth works part-time.

Elizabeth is not in the office all day, but she is very busy when she is there. Her job has many duties. For example, she answers the telephone and takes messages. She types letters for the director of the school. She orders supplies for the school. She files student information. She also helps the students.

The files have important information
about each student in them.

The telephone is an important part of Elizabeth's job. Many people call the school. They want information about the school. Sometimes these callers want to learn English at the school, or they want a friend to learn English.

"When are the classes?   Where is the school?   How much are the classes? How do I get a visa?''

Elizabeth answers these questions many times. Sometimes people call the school because they want information. But they only speak a little English. They are nervous. Elizabeth is very friendly on the telephone. She speaks slowly. She answers the questions. She is kind to the people on the telephone. People like the school because they like Elizabeth. She is very helpful. Her job is very important.

Elizabeth does other things, too. She types letters for the director. She is a good typist. She can type very fast. Elizabeth orders supplies for the school. For example, she orders pencils, pens, notebooks, and paper for the teachers. In addition, Elizabeth must keep the student files in order. Each student has a file. The file has all the important information about the student in it. It has the student's address and telephone number. It has the student's grades and a record of classes. Elizabeth puts the files in a filing cabinet. The files are in alphabetical order by last name.

Elizabeth helps students to fill out registration forms.

Another important duty for Elizabeth is helping the students. She helps them find their classrooms. She helps them find their books. Sometimes she takes them to the nurse when they feel sick. Elizabeth only works four hours every day, but she is very busy. She is very important.

Elizabeth likes her job. She likes to meet students from all over the world. The students like Elizabeth. She is kind to them. But many students are surprised to see her. Elizabeth is not young. She looks like a grandmother. She has white hair. She is in her 70s. The students are surprised. Why does she work?

Elizabeth enjoys her work. She enjoys the students. She is like a grandmother with many children from many countries. The students like to talk to her. They tell her about their homes. They tell her about their problems. For example, sometimes they miss their homes and families. They tell Elizabeth, and they feel better. Elizabeth is a good listener. Elizabeth tells the students about her family. She shows them pictures of her grandchildren. Elizabeth likes the students, and they like her, too.

Elizabeth likes to work. She wants to work. She doesn't feel old. "Just because you reach a certain age, you don't have to stop working," Elizabeth says. "I am healthy and I like working. When I'm older maybe I will retire and live with one of my children," she says. "I don't want anyone taking care of me when I can take care of myself." Elizabeth is very independent. "If I can work and enjoy it—why not?" she says.

AFTER READING

Questions 1–5 all need the answer *yes* or *no.* The answers can be short. For example: *Does the alphabet have 26 letters? Yes, it does.* Or the answers can be long. For example: *Is your teacher from Taiwan? No, she isn't from Taiwan. She's from the United States.*

Answer each question. If you answer *no,* give a long answer with the correct information.

1. Is Elizabeth a teacher?

    _____

2. Are the students at the school foreigners?

    _____

3. Is Elizabeth a full-time secretary?

    _____

4. Does Elizabeth answer the telephone?

    _____

5. Do the students like Elizabeth?

    _____

Can you write three yes/no questions about the reading?

1. _____

2. _____

3. _____

These questions are different. They are not yes/no questions. These questions begin with question words. These words ask for information. The answer to these questions must be information. The question word *why* wants a **reason** to be the answer. For example: *Why do you have an umbrella?* (What is the reason?) *Because it is raining.*

Answer these questions about the reading with the correct information.

1. Why do people call the school?

   _____

2. What are three things that Elizabeth does at work?

   _____

3. How many hours does Elizabeth work each day?

   _____

4. How old is Elizabeth?

   _____

5. Why does Elizabeth work?

   _____

Exercise 3

Do this activity in pairs or small groups. Imagine you are Hue Truong. You go to the English language school and talk to Elizabeth. You want some information about the school. What questions do you want to ask Elizabeth?

1. _____

2. _____

3. _____

4. _____

5. _____

Imagine you are Elizabeth. Hue Truong is visiting you and asking information about the school. What information do you need from Hue? What questions do you want to ask her?

6. _____

7. _____

8. _____

9. _____

10. _____

Now, role-play this situation with your partner or group.

Exercise 4

What is an **example**? It gives ideas to help you understand a word or phrase.

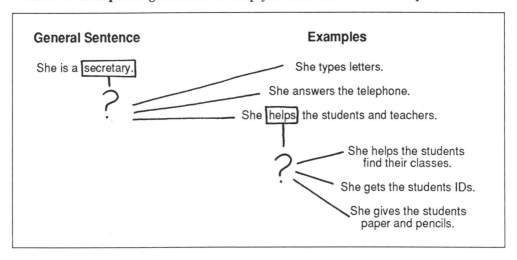

In a reading, a statement is often followed with examples to help you understand.
Find examples of the following things in the reading:

| Questions People Ask Elizabeth | Supplies | Reasons Elizabeth Likes Her Job |

Look at the sentences below. They are very general. Complete each sentence by giving examples that will help a person understand the sentence.

1. I like many kinds of foods. For example, I like _____, _____,

   and _____.

2. There are many interesting sports. For example, _____, _____,

   and _____ are interesting.

3. He is a very good student. For example, he comes to class on time,

   _____, and _____.

Exercise 5

Here are some words from the reading: *I, you, he, she, it, we, they, me, her,* and *them.* They are **pronouns.** It is important to know the word or group of words the pronoun refers to. For example, look at these sentences:

> The student is buying a book. **It** is for an English class.

The word *it* refers to the word *book* in the first sentence (it = the book). The second sentence could also be *The book is for an English class.*

Write down the noun that each pronoun refers to.

1. Elizabeth is a secretary at a language school. **It** is an English school.

   it = _____

2. There are also many teachers at the school. **They** teach English.

   they = _____

3. Many people call the school. **They** want information about **it.**

   they = _____

   it = _____

4. Each student has a file. **It** has all the important information about the student in it.

   it = _____

5. The students like Elizabeth. **She** is kind to **them.**

   she = _____

   them = _____

6. Sometimes Elizabeth takes the students to the nurse when **they** feel sick.

   they = _____

7. ''**I** don't want anyone taking care of **me** when I can take care of myself,'' Elizabeth says.

   I = _____

me = _____

8. Elizabeth likes her job. **It** is interesting.

   it = _____

9. The students like Elizabeth. "**We** like **her**," they say.

   we = _____

   her = _____

10. Elizabeth has two daughters. **They** do not live with her.

    they = _____

    her = _____

Exercise 6

Complete each sentence with the correct word from the list.

hours	teacher	foreign	student
information	dinner	rings	retire
secretary	lunch	important	jobs

1. Elizabeth Carr is a _____.

2. Most Americans eat _____ at 6:00 P.M.

3. The telephone _____ a lot at the office.

4. The students all come from _____ countries.

5. A secretary, a teacher, and a nurse are all examples of _____.

6. Most people work eight _____ a day at their jobs.

7. Usually workers _____ from their jobs when they turn 65 years old.

8. _____ is the meal in the middle of the day.

9. Elizabeth gives them _____ about the school.

10. The _____ gives the students homework every night.

Exercise 7—Word Study

Look at these words:

Verb	Noun	Definition
teach	teacher	a person who teaches
write	writer	a person who writes
drive	driver	a person who drives

The -er changes the word from a verb to a noun.
   The word changes meaning from an action to a person who does the action.

   Can you finish this list?

Verb	Noun	Definition
sing	_____	_____
manage	_____	_____
dance	_____	_____
play	_____	_____
swim*	_____	_____
run*	_____	_____

*These have a spelling change.

   Other endings are -or and -ist. These are also for people.

Verb	Noun	Definition
direct	director	a person who directs
act	actor	a person who acts
guitar	guitarist	a person who plays the guitar
type	typist	a person who types

What is a person who plays the violin? _____
We use the ending -er for things.
A pencil sharpener is a thing that sharpens pencils.
A heater is a thing that heats.
A computer is a machine that computes.
A coffee maker is a machine that makes coffee.

Endings can help us understand words in a reading.

Now, look at the reading "Elizabeth Carr: A Very Important Person." Find five words in the reading that use the endings *-er, -or,* and *-ist* to mean a person or thing that does something.

BE CAREFUL!!!! Some words end in *-er* but do not mean "a person who..." *Letter* and *dinner* are examples. Write the words below.

1. _____   2. _____   3. _____

4. _____   5. _____

READING HELPERS

There are many things that can help you read and understand. For example, every sentence gives you an idea. What is a sentence? You can recognize sentences because they begin with a capital letter and end with a **punctuation mark.** An end punctuation mark can be a period (.), a question mark (?), or an exclamation point (!).

Many sentences together make a paragraph. The first line of a paragraph is **indented.** This means it is moved in from the left-hand side of the page. Each paragraph has a **main idea.** All the sentences in the paragraph give information about this one idea.

Many paragraphs together make up a reading. Chapter 2 has a reading about Elizabeth. Each paragraph gives you more information about Elizabeth. How many paragraphs are there on this page?

Before you begin, you can get ideas about the reading. The first helper in a reading is the **title.** The title is the name for the reading. Always read the title before you read. It will help you get ready to read. You also know that pictures can help you. Under the pictures you can often find **captions.** A caption is a sentence or two about the picture.

Capital letters can also help you when you read. They show you when a sentence is beginning. And they show you when a word is a name. You use capital letters for names. *In the reading you meet Elizabeth Carr.* Notice the capital E and the capital C in this sentence. These words are not starting the sentence, so that tells you that they are names. Look at this sentence: *She is Elizabeth Carr from Texas.* There are three names in this sentence.

There are many things that can help you when you read: capital letters, punctuation marks, the title, and captions are just a few. Recognizing sentences and paragraphs can also help you. Look for them when you read.

MORE READING

Supplemental Reading 3—"A Letter Home"
Supplemental Reading 4—"Elizabeth's Family"
Supplemental Reading 5—"Mike Gets an Apartment"

Chapter 3
Looking for Adventure

GETTING IDEAS

1. What can you see in this picture?
2. What is happening in the picture?
3. Do people climb mountains in your country?
4. What are some other sports like climbing?

BUILDING IDEAS

Going somewhere new and exciting is an adventure. Doing something new and exciting is an adventure. Adventures are sometimes dangerous. Let's build ideas about adventures. What are some examples of adventures? Where do people go for adventures? Why do people go on adventures?

adventure

Many times mountain climbing is an adventure. It is an exciting sport, and it is often dangerous. What are some of the dangers of mountain climbing? How does a mountain climber go up a mountain safely? How does a mountain climber come down a mountain safely?

mountain climbing

GETTING READY TO READ

Exercise 1

Many words have **opposites.** For example, the opposite of *black* is *white,* and the opposite of *left* is *right.* Do you know the opposites of these words? Talk about these words with your class.

1. up   _____

2. brother   _____

3. stop   _____

4. high   _____

5. young   _____

6. top   _____

7. good   _____

8. east   _____

9. tall   _____

Exercise 2

Sometimes you can understand what you are reading by looking at the pictures in the reading. The pictures can help you understand the words. Read each set of sentences. Then match the picture with the sentence. The boldfaced word will help you find the correct picture. Write the number of the picture in the blank.

_____   1.   Gloria and Sam like the mountains. They also like snow. They enjoy **skiing** in the winter.

_____   2.   John likes the excitement of jumping out of planes. He likes **sky diving** very much.

_____   3.   Jill enjoys rivers. She likes fast rivers. **Kayaking** is a good sport for her.

_____   4.   Every year, Mark goes to Mexico. He likes **snorkeling** in the ocean and looking at the fish in the water.

_____   5.   Robert and Susan like to **jog.** They run every morning before work.

_____ 6. Tom and Mike like going up the mountain, but **rappelling** down the mountain is very dangerous.

_____ 7. Every summer Tom goes **hiking,** or **backpacking,** in the country. It is very quiet. He enjoys these long walks alone.

_____ 8. I like **camping** with my family. I like sleeping in a tent at night.

_____ 9. **Fishing** is a good sport. After you stop, you can eat the fish for dinner.

Exercise 3

Look at the picture. Complete each sentence with the correct word or phrase from the list.

on   above   at the top of   up
in   below   at the bottom of   down

1. The men are _____ the mountain.

2. A tent is _____ the mountain.

3. Tom is looking _____ at Mike.

4. Mike is looking _____ at Tom.

5. Tom's ice ax is _____ the snow.

6. A flag is _____ the mountain.

7. Mike is _____ Tom.

8. Tom is _____ Mike.

Exercise 4

Sentences give us information. Read each sentence and talk about the information in it with your class.

1. Mike and Tom Carr have the same birthday.
2. They are on the tennis team and the track team.
3. They are on the ski team at college.
4. They like mountain climbing because it is challenging.
5. They want to climb the high mountains in Peru.
6. At the time of the accident, Mike and Tom are coming down the mountain.
7. Tom tries to stop Mike, but he can't.
8. It takes them about two hours to hike to the road.

LET'S GO

Look at the title of the reading, and look at the pictures and captions. What do you think the reading is about?
    As you read, think about the answers to these questions:

1. What sports do Tom and Mike like?
2. Where does the accident happen?
3. Why does the accident happen?
4. Is anyone injured?
5. Is the ending happy or sad?

——————————— Are you ready to read? ———————————

Mike

Tom

An Accident in the Mountains

Mike and Tom Carr are twin brothers. They are the same age, have the same birthday, and look the same, too. They do many things together. They work together, live together, and play together.

Mike and Tom Carr like many sports. For example, they like skiing and running. They like learning about new and exciting sports. They like adventures, too. They like mountain climbing very much. They like it because it is challenging. They like the adventure.

How did they get interested in sports? Why do they like mountain climbing? Let's look at who they are.

It is 1956. Mike and Tom are three years old. They are learning to ski. Their father can ski, and he is a very good skier. He is teaching them to ski. They like skiing, and they ski every year. Soon they are very good skiers.

Mike and Tom learn to ski when they are three years old.

They are young, and they like sports. In elementary school, they play tennis and soccer. In junior high school, they are on the soccer team. They also like running, so they are on the track team. In high school, they run on the cross-country team in the fall and the track team in the spring. And every winter they ski.

After high school, Mike and Tom both go to college. They are on the ski team. They ski very well, and they win many races. But after two years they want some new adventures. They quit the ski team and begin to do some challenging things on skis. For example, they ski off high cliffs of snow and jump down 60 feet to more snow below. They ski jump over cars and trucks. They are having fun, and they are having adventures. But they are also having accidents. They go to the doctor a lot.

They both get jobs after college, but their main interest is still adventure. One day, their younger brother, Rick, invites Tom and Mike to go mountain climbing. They like it very much. It is exciting and dangerous. Mike is afraid of high places, but he likes climbing. It is a challenge. They climb a lot of high mountains in the United States. Soon they want to climb high mountains in other countries, too.

It is 1985. Mike and Tom go to Peru for three weeks. They want to climb four high mountains in western Peru. Many mountains are over 19,000 feet (6,000 meters). First, they climb the tallest mountain. It is 22,205 feet (6,768 meters) high. Then they climb two other high moutains. They are getting tired, but they have one more mountain to climb.

Mike and Tom camp for the night on Chacraraju. They can see the highest mountain in Peru, Huascaran, in the distance.

Mike and Tom hike for two days to get to the bottom of Chacraraju. This mountain is 20,047 feet (6,110 meters) high. They don't think the climb is going to be difficult. But there's something they don't know. The nickname for this mountain is "The Impossible Peak." Many climbers want to go to the top of Chacraraju. However, most of them cannot reach the top because the mountain has a steep, 3,000-foot (914 meters) face to climb. It is too difficult for most climbers.

Mike and Tom do not have a lot of time. They want to climb the mountain in two days. They climb for nine hours on the first day. It is a long day, and they are tired. They sleep on the mountain. It is beautiful. The next day, at 6:00 in the morning, they begin to climb again. They climb for many hours. Finally, they reach the top of the 3,000-foot face. The climb is a success. At 3:30 in the afternoon, they start to climb down the mountain.

It takes a long time to climb down a mountain, too. Many climbers tie a rope at the top and come down the mountain on the rope. This is called rappelling. But sometimes the rope does not stay at the top. Sometimes the rope pulls out, and this is very dangerous. "Many accidents happen when people are rappelling," Mike says.

The route up the mountain was difficult.

At the time of the accident, Mike and Tom are coming down the 3,000-foot face of the mountain. They are halfway down the mountain. But something is wrong with the rope, and they have to stop. Mike climbs back up to fix the rope. Tom is standing below. Mike is fixing the rope. Suddenly, the rope at the top pulls out, but Mike doesn't know it. Mike begins to come back down, but there is nothing holding the rope. He begins to fall down the mountain. He is falling down, and he is screaming. Tom looks up and sees his brother falling. He tries to stop Mike, but he can't.

Tom and Mike are tied together. Mike falls, and his rope pulls Tom off the mountain. Now they are both falling. Sometimes they hit the side of the mountain. It hurts to hit the hard ice and rock. "The next time I hit, I hope I die," Mike is thinking. He wants to stop falling. He wants the pain to stop. "The next time I hit, I should try to stop," Tom thinks. But he can't do anything because they are falling so fast. They are falling 1,500 feet down the mountain.

Finally, they stop. They are about 50 feet apart. At first, they do not know that the other person is all right. Mike sits up after he stops falling. "I'm alive!" he thinks. He is surprised. Then Mike hears a sound. He turns around and sees Tom.

"Mike, are you OK?" Tom asks.

"How did you get down here?" Mike says.

"I fell, too," Tom tells him.

For a few minutes they just sit and look at each other. They are both hurt, but they are alive.

The road is about six miles (10 kilometers) away. There is no one there to help them. Mike and Tom both hurt their right knees. They can't walk well. They slowly walk four miles to a trail. It is about midnight, so they make a place to sleep for the night.

The next morning, they hike to the road. It takes them about two hours to walk two miles. At the road, they stop a truck. They want to go to Huaraz. This is the main city in this part of Peru. Mike and Tom rest in Huaraz for a week after their fall. Then they return to the United States. Soon they are ready to climb another mountain. They like the adventure and danger.

Mike and Tom are ready to climb
another mountain.

AFTER READING

Write T if the sentence is true (right) and F if the sentence is false (wrong). If the sentence is false, rewrite it with the correct information.

_____ 1. Mike and Tom live together.

_____

_____ 2. Their father doesn't ski.

_____

_____ 3. They learned to ski in junior high school.

_____

_____ 4. Rappelling is not easy.

_____

_____ 5. The accident happens in Peru.

_____

_____ 6. They fall 3,000 feet.

_____

_____ 7. Tom breaks his leg.

_____

Answer the questions with short answers.

1. Who takes Tom and Mike mountain climbing the first time?

_____

2. What is the name of the mountain with the 3,000-foot face?

_____

3. Why is the mountain's nickname "The Impossible Peak"?

_____

4. Why does Mike fall?

_____

5. How far must they walk to the road?

_____

Exercise 3

Imagine you are a newspaper reporter. You are interviewing Mike and Tom Carr about their accident in Peru. Write down five yes/no questions you want to ask them.

1. _____

2. _____

3. _____

4. _____

5. _____

Write down five *wh-* questions (information questions) you want to ask them.

6. _____

7. _____

8. _____

9. _____

10. _____

Now role-play this situation in class. Two students are Mike and Tom, and the other students are reporters. The reporters choose the questions they want to ask. "Mike" and "Tom" try to answer the questions.

Exercise 4

This reading tells us about Mike and Tom by using time. Sometimes you can remember what you read by putting the facts onto a **timeline.** You can remember the important information in the reading by organizing it according to time.

The left side of the timeline below answers the question *when.* Add information to the right side. This information answers the question *what.* What sports are Tom and Mike doing each time?

A Growing Interest in Sports

When?	What Sport?
1956	Mike and Tom learn to ski.
elementary school	
junior high school	
high school	
college	
after college	

Add the missing information to the timeline below.

An Accident in the Mountains

When?	What Happens?
Before Climb	Hike for ___ days to bottom of mountain.
Day One	Climb for ___ hours.
	Sleep on mountain.
Day Two	Begin to climb at ___ A.M.
	Reach top of ___ foot face.
	Begin to climb down at ___ P.M.
	Fall down ___ feet after rope pulls loose.
	Hike ___ miles to trail.
	Make a camp and go to sleep at ___ .
Day Three	Hike ___ miles to road in ___ hours.
	Hitch a ride to the city of ___ .
End of Trip	Leave ___ after ___ days.

Exercise 5

There are many words for people in a family.

mother	son	aunt
father	daughter	uncle
parents	child	cousin
grandmother	children	sister
grandfather	twins	brother
grandparents	only child	grandchildren

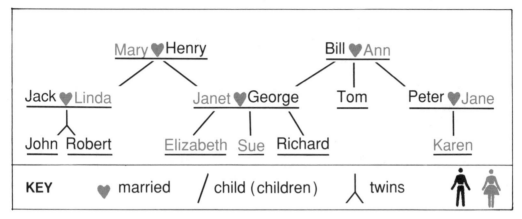

Look at the family tree above. Talk about the people in this family tree. Then complete each sentence with the correct word from the list.

1. Linda and Janet are _____.

2. Janet and George are the _____ of Sue, Richard, and Elizabeth.

3. Mary and Henry have two _____.

4. Bill and Ann have three _____.

5. John and Robert are Karen's _____.

6. Bill and Ann are Karen's _____.

7. Mary and Henry have five _____.

8. John and Robert are _____.

9. Elizabeth and Sue have one _____. His name is Richard.

10. Peter and Jane have one _____.

Exercise 6—Word Study

Adjectives are important words. An adjective gives you more information about a noun. For example, colors are adjectives.

> The mountain is **white.**

This sentence tells you the color of the mountain. You can imagine a white mountain. You can guess there is snow on the mountain.

Look at these sentences:

> Tom and Mike like to climb mountains.
> Tom and Mike like to climb **high** mountains.

The word **high** is an adjective. It give you more information about the mountain. It helps you imagine the mountain. It *describes* the mountain.

Look at these examples:

> an **impossible** peak   a **dangerous** sport   an **easy** climb

The words *impossible, dangerous,* and *easy* are all adjectives. Each word gives you some more information about the noun.

Can you think of a noun to complete each phrase below?

1. a red _____

2. a blue _____

3. a green _____

4. a high _____

5. an easy _____

6. a small _____

7. a fat _____

8. a good _____

9. a big _____

10. a happy _____

Exercise 7—Word Study

Many times you can see an adjective in front of a noun. But sometimes the adjective is after the *be* verb. Look at these examples:

> The mountain is **white.**
> Today is **hot.**
> The climb is **difficult.**
> It is **beautiful** at the top.

Complete these sentences with an adjective.

1. Mike and Tom's father is a _____ skier.

2. The mountains are very _____.

3. They like _____ sports.

4. It is a _____ fall.

5. Mike hits the _____ ice and rock.

READING HELPERS

Many times in a reading you see these marks: " " These are **quotation marks.** These marks are important signals to a reader. Sometimes they show you the title of a reading. However, they usually show the exact words of a conversation. Any words that are inside these marks are the exact words someone says.

Do you remember Hue Truong? You can see these marks at the end of the reading about Hue. Look on page 7. What does Hue say? The quotation marks show the reader Hue's exact words.

Quotation marks in a reading allow you to **hear** the person talk.

Do you remember Elizabeth Carr? Look on page 18. Elizabeth is talking to the reader. What does she say? Her words are inside the quotation marks.

In the reading about Tom and Mike's accident, you can also find quotation marks. Look at the reading. What pages have quotations? Who is talking?

When you read, look for quotation marks. They help you hear the person talk.

MORE READING

Supplemental Reading 6—"Doing What You Want"
Supplemental Reading 7—"High Mountains of North America"

Chapter 4
Working on a River

GETTING IDEAS

1. What can you see in this picture?
2. What kind of boat is this?
3. Where is this boat?
4. Who works on this boat?

BUILDING IDEAS

What do you think of when you read about boats? Do you know the names of these kinds of boats? Where do they sail? Who uses them? Why do they use them? What moves them? Build your ideas below.

GETTING READY TO READ

Exercise 1

Verbs are important in sentences. A verb tells you the action in a sentence. Finding the verbs can help you understand the sentence. Do you know what verb to use in each sentence below? Can you guess?

1. I _____ music on the radio.

2. The boys _____ football every Saturday.

3. People _____ wood to keep warm in the winter.

4. This book _____ $22.00. It's expensive.

5. People _____ in a hotel.

6. On the boat, the passengers _____ good meals.

7. The college student _____ engineering.

8. A captain _____ a boat.

9. She _____ the piano very well.

10. It is nice to _____ in a chair and relax.

Exercise 2

Do you remember about capital letters? A capital letter can mean the word is a name. Look at this sentence: *She lives in Galena.*

The word *Galena* begins with a capital G, but it is not the first word in the sentence. It is a name. We see the words *lives in,* and we can guess that Galena is the name of a place.

Underline the names in the sentences below.

1. In the midwestern part of the United States, there are some long rivers.
2. The Mississippi River is a long river.
3. The *Julia Belle Swain* takes passengers on the Mississippi River from Le Claire, Iowa, to Chestnut Mountain Lodge near Galena, Illinois.
4. She lives in Miami.
5. The Smith family is going to Switzerland for a vacation.

Exercise 3

Look at the map on the next page and answer these questions.

1. What state are you in now? Can you find it on the map?
2. Where is the eastern part of the United States?
3. Where is the Midwest?
4. Where is the Mississippi River?
5. Where is the West?
6. Can you find Le Claire, Iowa, and Galena, Illinois?

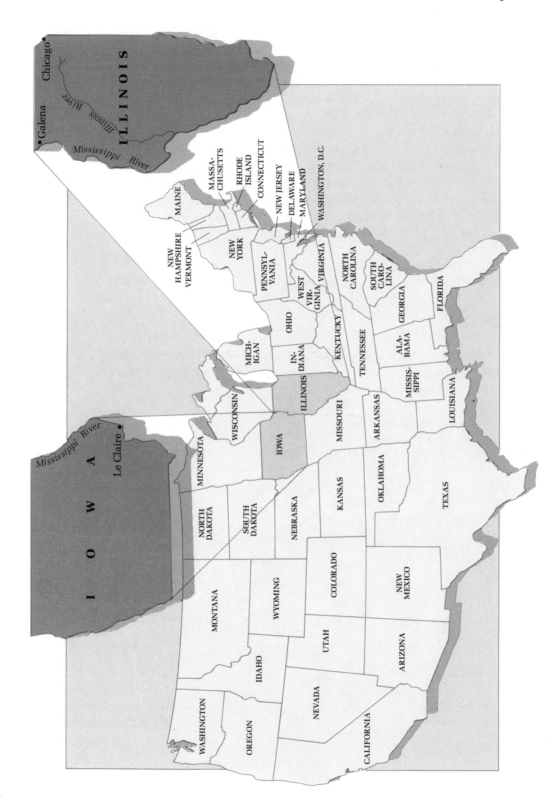

Exercise 4

What information do these sentences give us? Read each sentence and talk about the information in it with your class. Then look at the picture of the *Julia Belle Swain* at the beginning of the chapter. Label the parts of the boat on the picture.

1. The *Julia Belle Swain* is a river steamboat.
2. At the back of the boat is a large paddlewheel.
3. There are three decks, or floors, on the boat.
4. The pilothouse is a small room at the top of the boat.
5. There are two tall smokestacks in the front of the boat.
6. The *Julia Belle Swain* looks like it's old, but it's new.

Remember: Sentences give ideas to the reader. Read for ideas.

LET'S GO

Look at the title of the reading. Look at the pictures and read the captions. What do you think the reading is about? As you read, think about the answers to these questions about the boat:

1. How does the boat move?
2. What does the boat look like?
3. Who rides on the boat and why?

Then think about the answers to these questions about the captain:

4. Who is the captain?
5. What interesting things do you learn about the captain?
6. Does he like his job?

——————————— Are you ready to read? ———————————

The *Julia Belle Swain* and Her Captain

Dennis Trone is the captain of a river steamboat. The *Julia Belle Swain* is the name of the boat. It's not an old boat, but it looks like an old boat. It looks like a boat from 100 years ago.

The *Julia Belle Swain* has a large paddlewheel at its back. It turns around and around and pushes the boat through the water. A steam engine turns the paddlewheel. In old boats, wood or coal powered the engine, but today the boat burns oil. In front of the boat are two tall smokestacks. Smoke from the burning oil goes out these smokestacks. The oil heats water, and the water changes to steam. The steam moves the paddlewheel. This paddlewheel moves the boat down the river.

One hundred years ago, hundreds of steam-powered boats like the *Julia Belle Swain* carried passengers on the rivers of the United States. They traveled on the Mississippi River and the other important rivers of the Midwest, like the Missouri, Ohio, and Illinois rivers. Today we have airplanes, cars, buses, and trains. Now most boats carry cargo and use diesel engines. Not many boats carry passengers. There are not many riverboats for passengers. Only five of these boats are steam-powered. The *Julia Belle Swain* is one of these five steam-powered passenger boats in the United States today.

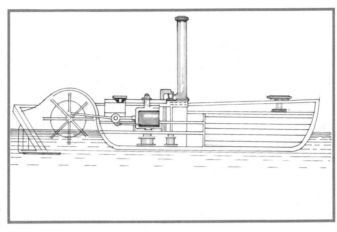

Steam makes the paddlewheel turn.

The *Julia Belle Swain* takes passengers on the Mississippi River from Le Claire, Iowa, to a hotel on the river near Galena, Illinois. The name of the hotel is the Chestnut Mountain Lodge. The passengers sleep in the hotel. On the next day, they visit Galena and return to Le Claire on the boat.

The boat moves slowly up and down the river. The ride is very peaceful because the boat's top speed is only 12 miles per hour. On the boat the people enjoy the view, eat good meals, and listen to bluegrass music. This is a traditional kind of music from the eastern part of the United States. Bluegrass music uses guitars, banjos, fiddles, and other instruments. The trip is slow and relaxing. People can rest. They can get away from the busy life of the city. They can talk with their friends. They can play games, and they can watch the beautiful country.

Passengers can enjoy good meals on their trip.

The boat is 156 feet long and 27 feet wide. It can carry 325 passengers. There are three decks, or floors. The second and third decks have inside rooms, and the first deck is open. Passengers may sit at tables, or they may lie back in deck chairs and relax. There are two dining rooms and a snack bar.

At the top of the boat is a box-like building with big windows on all four sides. This room at the top of the boat is the pilothouse. Captain Dennis Trone works here. From the pilothouse, Captain Trone can see in all directions. He steers the boat with a large, wooden steering wheel. In the pilothouse there is a two-way radio. The captain uses the radio to listen to weather reports, to talk to other boats, and to call for help in case of trouble.

Captain Trone likes his job. He started his passenger business on the *Julia Belle Swain* in 1971. Before he was a steamboat captain, he studied boat building and design. From 1948 to 1963 he was in the United States Navy. He likes boats very much.

Captain Trone grew up near the Illinois River. As a child he watched riverboats go down the river. "Some kids wanted to be cowboys. Some kids wanted to be baseball players. Some kids wanted to be movie stars. I just wanted to be a steamboat captain," he says.

Captain Trone pilots the boat through
a narrow part of the river.

The job of captain is not easy. A river steamboat captain must know the river like the back of his hand. This means he must know everything about the river. He must know where the river is deep and where it is shallow. He must know where the river is wide and where it is narrow. He must know where the river water goes fast and where it goes slow.

Weather can cause problems for the boat. High winds can turn the large, flat-bottomed boat around. Rain and fog sometimes hide the riverbanks and other boats. When the river water is low, the boat can hit the bottom. When the river water is high, the river becomes fast and dangerous.

"Piloting a steamboat is not very dangerous or difficult," says Captain Trone, "but the pilot must pay close attention. In some ways, it is like piloting an airplane. One mistake can bring disaster."

Because a mistake can be very serious, it takes a long time to become a riverboat pilot. Like a car driver, a pilot must have a license. When a person wants to become a riverboat pilot, the person usually begins as a deckhand on the boat. A deckhand helps keep the boat clean, helps with the ropes when the boat lands, and does many small jobs on the boat.

After this experience, the person becomes a trainee, someone who is training to be a riverboat pilot. A licensed pilot will supervise the trainee. When the pilot is watching, the trainee may steer the boat in safe places. Step by step, the pilot teaches the trainee to do more difficult steering. The trainee must learn to get the boat away from shore, to pass other boats, and to land the boat. After two years or more of training with a pilot, the trainee must take a test to get a pilot's license.

Captain Trone is a good captain. He's a safe captain. He has many years of experience as a steamboat pilot. However, he remembers one time when he almost had an accident. "When I was younger, I was piloting the *Julia Belle Swain* south of Peoria on the Illinois River. It was during the summer dry season, and the river was very low. I was coming to a very narrow part of the river. I saw a very large diesel towboat. It was pushing 15 barges full of coal. They weighed about 23,000 tons. I knew I had to pass very close to the towboat. The propellers of the towboat were nine feet wide. They made a very big whirlpool in the shallow water. The *Julia Belle Swain* turned completely around. She almost hit the barges. The boat was safe, but she almost had an accident," says Captain Trone. "I didn't have the experience. I didn't know the river well. Now, of course, I know what to do when this happens."

Towboats push barges on the river.

"Working on a steamboat or any riverboat is an adventurous life," says Captain Trone, "but it's not for everyone. It takes people away from home for long periods of time." Captain Trone has a large family. He's married and has five children. He takes his family with him on the *Julia Belle Swain.*

Dennis Trone is not the only steamboat pilot in his family. His son, Robert Trone, is a pilot now, too. In fact, everyone in the captain's family helps to run the boat. Running the boat is a family business. Captain Trone's wife, Libby, is a schoolteacher, but in the summertime she plays music for the passengers. She plays the boat's calliope, an organ that makes music with the boat's steam. His daughter, Lisa Trone, is now the business director of the steamboat company. The Trones' three other daughters also work on the boat in the summer.

Years ago, when he was a child, Dennis Trone knew that he wanted to be a steamboat captain. He's not sorry. The river and the steamboat give his family a good life.

AFTER READING

Exercise 1

Write T if the sentence is true (right) and F if the sentence if false (wrong). If the sentence is false, rewrite it with the correct information.

_____ 1. The *Julia Belle Swain* is a river steamboat.

_____

_____ 2. There are hundreds of passenger steamboats in the United States today.

_____

_____ 3. The *Julia Belle Swain* sails on the Illinois River from Le Claire, Iowa, to Galena, Illinois.

_____

_____

_____ 4. The passengers sleep on the boat.

_____

_____ 5. The boat's steering wheel is in the pilothouse on top of the boat.

_____

_____ 6. Dennis Trone is the captain of the *Julia Belle Swain.*

_____

_____ 7. Captain Trone began his passenger business in 1972.

_____

_____ 8. When Captain Trone was a child, he wanted to be a baseball player.

_____

Chapter 4

Exercise 2

Answer the questions with the correct information.

1. What do passengers do on the boat?

    _____

2. What did Captain Trone do before he was the captain?

    _____

3. What must a riverboat captain know about the river?

    _____

4. What are some weather problems for the captain?

    _____

5. How is piloting a riverboat like piloting an airplane?

    _____

6. What do Robert, Libby, and Lisa Trone do on the boat?

    _____

Exercise 3

Imagine that you and your family or you and a group of friends want to take a trip on the *Julia Belle Swain.* Fill in the application form below after you have looked at the information about the fares and dates.

FILL OUT AND MAIL WITH PAYMENT TO:

RIVER CRUISES

P.O. Box 406 • Galena, Illinois 61036
(815) 777-1660
Toll Free in Illinois: 1-800-237-1660
Outside Illinois: 1-800-331-1467

NAME _____

ADDRESS _____

CITY/STATE/ZIP _____

PHONE: Home ( ) _____ Office ( ) _____

TRIP DATE _____ NO. OF ADULTS _____ $160 EACH

NO OF CHILDREN (10-14) _____ $90 EACH   NO OF CHILDREN (under 10) _____ $60 EACH

TOTAL AMOUNT (Add $15 for each person in single room) _____

Please attach a sheet of paper with the names of all persons in your party and indicate who will share a lodge room. Does anyone in your party have a walking disability?

A TWO-DAY CRUISE ABOARD THE
JULIA BELLE SWAIN

DEPARTURES DAILY MAY 24 to OCTOBER 30
1st Day: Depart Le Claire 9:00 A.M. Arrive Chestnut Mountain 7:00 P.M.
2nd Day: Depart Chestnut Mountain 12:00 Noon. Arrive Le Claire 7:00 P.M.

RIVER CRUISES

P.O. Box 406
Galena, Illinois 61036
(815) 777-1660

Toll Free in Illinois:
1-800-237-1660
Outside Illinois:
1-800-331-1467

REFUNDS FOR
CANCELLATIONS
Less than 30 days—$25
per person not refunded
Less than 72 hours—
50% refund
Less than 24 hours—
no refund

Passengers board at the
Public Boat Landing at
Le Claire, Iowa.

CRUISE FARES

Includes All Meals
Activities • Lodging
$160.00 per person
(2 to 4 people per room)
$175.00 per person
(single room)
Child 10-14—$90.00
Child under 10—$60.00
Infant (crib rate)—$15.00

All passage must be reserved in advance. No fares transacted at the boarding point.

Please fill out the attached reservation form and mail with your check or money order.

CRUISE TIPS

Dress: The cruise is casual so sportswear is most appropriate. Comfortable shoes are a good idea.

Baggage: We recommend one medium-size piece of luggage and a carry-on bag per passenger. We will take the luggage from you at the boarding point; it will be taken by van to Chestnut Mountain Resort. Only hand-held bags may be brought aboard.

Parking: Overnight parking is available near the boat landing. Certain local hotels provide overnight parking and courtesy shuttle service to the boat landing.

Boarding Time: 8:30 A.M. We will have coffee, sweet rolls, milk, and fruit juice waiting for you.

When we send you your tickets, we will include a map of the Le Claire area and a list of local hotels and motels.

Exercise 4

A **fact** is something that is true. For example, this sentence is a fact: *George Washington was the first president of the United States.* This information is true.

An **opinion** is someone's idea about something. For example, this sentence is not a fact: *George Washington was the best president.* This is someone's opinion. It may or may not be another person's opinion. When we read, it is important to know the difference between fact and opinion.

Read the following sentences. Are these facts from the reading or opinions about the reading? Circle the correct answer.

1.	The *Julia Belle Swain* is a steamboat.	fact	opinion
2.	The Mississippi River is the best river.	fact	opinion
3.	Only five passenger boats in the United States are steam powered.	fact	opinion
4.	Taking a trip on the *Julia Belle Swain* is a lot of fun.	fact	opinion
5.	A trip on the *Julia Belle Swain* is expensive.	fact	opinion
6.	Dennis Trone is the captain.	fact	opinion

Exercise 5

There are different ways to remember the important information in a reading. For example, there are a number of important facts to remember from this reading. Fill in the following chart to help you remember the facts about the *Julia Belle Swain.*

JULIA BELLE SWAIN

TRIP FACTS

Boat Name: _____

Captain: _____

Top Speed: _____

Number of Passengers: _____

Number of Days: _____

From (city's name): _____

To (city's name): _____

Cost per Adult: _____

Sometimes important information in a reading explains how to do something. You want to remember each step in the process. Write down the steps in the processes on the next page:

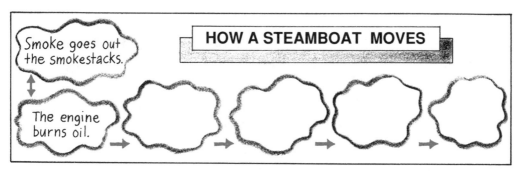

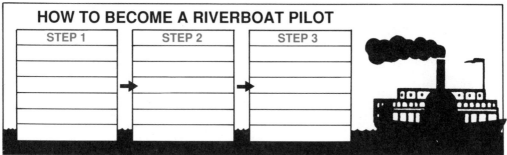

Exercise 6

Match the adjective in the left column with its opposite in the right column.

1. _____ big   a. bottom

2. _____ back   b. difficult

3. _____ top   c. shallow

4. _____ slow   d. small

5. _____ good   e. narrow

6. _____ inside   f. front

7. _____ easy   g. low

8. _____ deep   h. bad

9. _____ wide   i. safe

10. _____ high   j. fast

11. _____ dangerous   k. outside

Exercise 7—Word Study

Some of the words in this story are two words put together. These words are called **compound words.** For example, the compound word *steamboat* is the words *steam* + *boat* put together. It is a boat, and it uses steam to move.

Below is a list of words from the reading. What two words make up each word? Talk about the meanings of these words with your class.

1. riverboat   = _____

2. pilothouse   = _____

3. paddlewheel   = _____

4. smokestacks   = _____

5. deckhand   = _____

6. towboat   = _____

There are some other compound words you know. What two words make up each of these words below? Talk about the meanings with your class.

7. classroom   = _____

8. notebook   = _____

9. homework   = _____

10. homesick   = _____

11. headache   = _____

12. bookcase   = _____

13. suitcase   = _____

READING HELPERS

When you do not know a word, you sometimes use a dictionary. A bilingual dictionary gives a translation of a word. An English-English dictionary gives the meaning of a word. This explanation of the meaning of a word is called a **definition.**
    You do not always need your dictionary. Sometimes you can find the definition

of a new word from the reading. Watch for these signals after the new word. They often tell you that the writer is giving you the definition of a word.

1. The verb *to be*

> Bluegrass music **is** a traditional kind of music from the eastern part of the United States.

What is bluegrass music? *Is* tells you that *a traditional kind of music from the eastern part of the United States* is a definition of bluegrass music.

2. The verb *means*

> A river steamboat captain must know the river like the back of his hand. This **means** he must know everything about the river.

What does *like the back of his hand* mean? The word *means* indicates a definition, in this case, *he must know everything about the river.*

3. A comma and the word *or*

> The boat has three decks, **or** floors.

What is a deck? The comma and the word *or* tell you that *floors* is another word for *decks*.

4. A comma

> Libby Trone plays the boat's calliope, an organ that makes music with the boat's steam.

What is a calliope? The comma tells you that the words *an organ that makes music with the boat's steam* give a definition of calliope.

Read this sentence:

> A deckhand can be a trainee, a person training to be a riverboat pilot.

What is a trainee? How do you do this?

MORE READING

Supplemental Reading 8—"A Journey Back in Time"
Supplemental Reading 9—"The Big Water"

Chapter 5
Working on an American Farm

GETTING IDEAS

1. What can you see in this picture?
2. What is growing here?
3. What do people do here?
4. Where is this farm?
5. What are farms like in your country?

BUILDING IDEAS

Do you like to live in the country or in the city? Life for a farm family is different from life for a city family. Talk about the differences with your class. Build your ideas here.

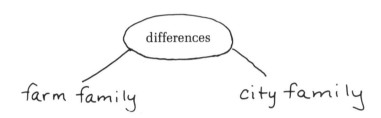

GETTING READY TO READ

Exercise 1

Circle the word that is the opposite of the boldfaced word on the left.

1.	**large**	big	low	small
2.	**young**	child	old	small
3.	**wet**	rain	water	dry
4.	**expensive**	good	cheap	high
5.	**country**	land	city	water
6.	**same**	different	like	some
7.	**more**	less	move	same
8.	**good**	nice	bad	kind
9.	**begin**	end	middle	start
10.	**outside**	beside	inside	outdoors
11.	**close**	next	far	near
12.	**buy**	pay	near	sell

There are more compound words in this reading. Remember, a compound word is two words put together. For example, in the last chapter we learned *steamboat, paddlewheel,* and *pilothouse.* What do you think the words below mean? Talk about the meanings of these words with your class.

1. farmhouse   =   _____

2. farmland   =   _____

3. landowner   =   _____

4. housework   =   _____

5. sunrise   =   _____

6. sunset   =   _____

Exercise 3

Sentences give us information. Read each sentence and talk about the information in it with your class.

1. In 1900, 38 percent of all Americans lived and worked on farms. Today only 2.2 percent of them live on farms.
2. Susan lived in the same house when she was young.
3. Four generations of her family lived in this house.
4. The family owns their house and the farm buildings, but they do not own the farmland. They rent the farmland.
5. On the farm they grow wheat, corn, and soybeans.
6. In addition, the family raises sheep.
7. Susan's husband Cecil studied raising animals at college.
8. Susan and her mother preserve the food from the garden. This means they put the food in glass jars, cover them tightly, and boil the jars. After this, it is safe to keep the food for a long time.

LET'S GO

Farmers work hard all year. Each season, the farmer is busy. What are the four seasons? What do you think farmers do in each season? What work do farmers do all year? Write your ideas on the next page.

_____

_____

_____

_____

The title of the reading is "The Graber Family: American Farmers." When you read, look for information about the work the Graber family does on their farm. What work didn't you write above? Underline this new information when you read.

———————— Are you ready to read? ————————

The Graber Family: American Farmers

In 1900, 38 percent of all Americans lived and worked on farms. Today, only 2.2 percent of them live on farms. What is life like for this small group of Americans?

Susan Graber is a member of a farm family. She lives on a farm in central Illinois. She lives in a big farmhouse with her husband and her daughter. Susan lived in this same house when she was young. Her father lived in this house when he was a boy. Susan's grandparents, her parents, her brothers, and her daughter have lived in this house. So four generations of Susan's family have lived in the same house.

Today Susan's parents live in a new house next door to the old farmhouse. Susan, her husband Cecil, and her daughter live in the old farmhouse. Susan, her husband, her father, and her mother work together on the farm. The men work in the fields with the machines and animals. Usually the women work in the house and garden.

The farm is 550 acres (2.2. square kilometers). The family owns the house and the farm buildings, but they do not own the farmland. They rent this land from a landowner. On the farm they grow wheat, corn, and soybeans. Corn and soybeans are the big crops. The family earns most of their money from the corn and soybeans. In addition, the family raises sheep. The sheep produce meat and wool.

Susan tells about the family's life on the farm. "Our farm today is different from farms in the past," says Susan. "In the past, farmers had a little bit of many things. They had cows, chickens, pigs, and sheep. They had several crops and large gardens for vegetables. Today, the farms in central Illinois are very specialized. Most farmers raise only two crops—corn and soybeans—and keep no animals."

"Our farm is unusual here," Susan says, "because we still have animals. My husband Cecil studied animals at college. He is very interested in animals and likes to take care of them. The animals take a lot of time. We have more work than other farmers here because of the sheep."

Spring is a busy time for all Illinois farmers. In April, when the weather is not too wet, the spring planting begins. The farmers plant the corn first. Three or four weeks later, they plant soybeans. When the seeds begin to grow, the farmers put chemical fertilizers on the soil. The fertilizers give the plants food. The food helps the plants to grow. When the plants are young, the farmers must kill the weeds in the fields. Weeds are plants that the farmers do not want. They use chemicals and machines to kill the weeds. Cecil and Susan's father work in the fields from sunrise to sunset.

Of course, the farmers have to eat, and it is Susan's job to prepare all of the family's meals. She begins her work with breakfast at 6 o'clock in the morning. In addition, she must do the housework and care for her daughter. She shares this work with her mother.

The women also take care of the family's large garden. The vegetables and fruit from the garden are for their own family, not for sale. In the spring, they plant the vegetables. All during the summer and fall they use the food from the garden for the family's meals. They preserve the food from the garden. This means they put the food in glass jars, cover them tightly, and boil the jars. After this, it is safe to keep the food for a long time. In the winter, they can eat applesauce, tomatoes, and corn that they preserved in the summer.

Cecil Graber feeds hay to the sheep.

Susan and her mother
preserve food
for the winter.

In the middle of the summer, many farmers have time to relax. The crops are growing. However, the Grabers also have animals. They need hay to feed the sheep in winter. Hay is dried grass. A machine cuts the grass and ties it together. Later, they store the hay in the barn for the winter. Usually they make hay four or five times in one summer.

Fall, or autumn, is another busy season for the farm. The farmers must gather the corn and soybeans. The corn and soybean harvest begins in September. This is one time when Susan helps in the fields. The farmers use a combine. This machine cuts the plants and separates the corn and beans from the rest of the plant. The combine pours the grain into a wagon in the field. It is Susan's job to drive the tractor that pulls this wagon.

Susan enjoys the harvest work. "I love that time of year," she says. "I can be outside. The weather is cool. I often have time to read in the tractor. And I don't have to worry about the meals. My mother makes the meals for all of us."

When the harvest ends, the farmers must sell their corn and soybeans. Cecil listens to the reports of corn and soybean prices on radio and television. He talks to other farmers. He wants to sell his grain for a good price. But this is not always easy. Maybe the prices will go up and he will make money. Maybe the prices will go down and he will lose money. He cannot be sure.

Farming is a business. Like other business people, farmers must keep careful records of their money. Susan does this job. She writes down all their expenses. Expenses are the things that a person pays money for. She also writes down their income. Income is the money that they get. "I often do this work in the evening. I do it after my daughter goes to bed," Susan says.

Susan keeps a record of their
income and expenses.

In the winter, the Grabers do not have to work in the fields. However, they cannot relax. In January, February, and March they work hard. The sheep have their lambs during these months. The family must stay close to care for the animals during this time.

The family is busy during all the seasons of the year, and they work hard and long. Susan does not like this part of living on a farm. "Because of the animals," she says, "we can't travel. We can't take a vacation. We have to be home mornings and evenings to feed the animals." Susan also dislikes another part of farming. She worries about the high risks. "Maybe we will have a good year, maybe a bad year. We never know. Good weather is important. Bad weather means a bad crop." Susan also worries about grain market prices. "We must pay for supplies—machines, seeds, chemicals, fertilizer, and fuels. We must pay the rent for the land. When the prices for grain on the market are too low, we cannot pay our expenses. We can never be sure about money," she says.

However, Susan likes another part of farming. "We are very independent here," she says. "No one tells us when to work or what to do. We are our own bosses. Of course, when we don't do the work, no one else will do it for us."

Susan also likes to live in the country, where she can see nature around her every day. "I lived in towns and cities before I married, but I didn't like it. There were always people close. I always needed more space," says Susan. "I think that was because I grew up on the farm, and I always had so much space around me. Neighbors were far away. I like the feeling of open space around me. I like to go for a walk where there are no cars and no other people close."

The Graber family farm
is in central Illinois.

Susan and her family are not sure about their future in farming. In 1987, 5.3 million Americans stopped farming. Many farm families stop farming because they lose money. The Graber family knows this. They worry about prices on the grain market. "Some people say that farms of the future will be bigger than today," says Susan. "That means bigger machines, longer hours, more money risk. Maybe farming will not be a family business in the future." Susan thinks that she and Cecil will stay in farming, but she is not sure about her daughter's future. She does not know if the big farmhouse will see another generation of children.

Chapter 5

AFTER READING

Did you remember to underline the Graber family's work in the reading? (Do this now if you forgot.) Add the new information to your list in the Let's Go section.

Exercise 2

Write T if the sentence is true (right) and F if the sentence is false (wrong). If the sentence is false, rewrite it with the correct information.

_____ 1. Every year more Americans move to farms.

_____

_____ 2. Susan lives with her father and mother in a farmhouse.

_____

_____ 3. Susan's parents work with her and Cecil on the farm.

_____

_____ 4. The Graber family rents the farmhouse.

_____

_____ 5. The Graber family farm has cows, chickens, and sheep.

_____

_____ 6. In the spring, the farmers harvest their crops.

_____

_____ 7. The Graber family cannot relax in the summer.

_____

_____ 8. Susan works in the field at harvest time.

_____

_____ 9. Susan dislikes harvest work.

_____

_____ 10. When harvest is over, Cecil watches television and listens to the radio because he wants to relax.

_____

_____

_____ 11. In the winter, the Graber family works very hard to take care of the sheep.

_____

_____ 12. People are not sure about the future of farm families in America.

_____

Exercise 3

The title of this reading is "The Graber Family: American Farmers." The reading tells us a little about all of the members of the Graber family, but it tells us a lot about Susan Graber. The information about Susan is a very important part of the reading. Answer these questions about Susan.

1. What are Susan's duties on the farm? Make a list of her duties.

_____

_____

_____

2. We can often remember important information from a reading by making lists of ideas from the reading. Do you think Susan is happy with her life? To answer this question, make two lists here about what Susan likes and dislikes.

Susan *likes* these things about her life on the farm.

_____

_____

_____

_____

Susan *dislikes* these things about her life on the farm.

_____

_____

_____

_____

Exercise 4

Complete each sentence with the correct word from the list.

risk	husband
generations	example
seasons	daughter
busy	weather
parents	different

1. Susan, her husband, her daughter, her mother, and her father live and work on

   the same farm. Three _____ of the family live and work together.

2. Susan's _____ live in a new house near the old farmhouse. She is
   happy because her mother and father live near her.

3. The name of Susan's _____ is Cecil. He studied raising animals at
   college. He likes to take care of animals.

4. Susan and Cecil have one _____. The girl's name is Sonya.

5. Susan fixes all the family's meals, plants the family garden, takes care of her
   child, does the housework, keeps records of the family expenses, and

   sometimes works in the fields. She is very _____.

6. Farms today are _____ from farms in the past. In the past, farms had
   many kinds of plants and animals. Today, most farms have only one or two
   kinds of plants and no animals.

7. Farmers in Illinois have a lot of work in the spring. For _____, they
   plant the corn and beans, fertilize the fields, and kill the weeds.

8. All Illinois farmers have a lot of work in the spring and fall. The Graber family

   has work in all four _____ of the year because they have animals.

9. Corn needs rain and sunshine. Too much rain or too little rain is bad for the

   corn. Wind storms can kill the corn. Good _____ is important for a
   good corn harvest.

10. Each year farmers take a _____. In a bad year, they may lose their
    money. In a good year, they may make money. They cannot be sure about
    money.

Exercise 5—Word Study

Read the two sentences below:

> In the spring the farmers plant the corn.
> Last spring the farmers planted the corn.

What is the difference in meaning between the two sentences? What is the verb in each sentence? How are the verbs different? The *-ed* ending on a verb tells us that the action happened in the past.

Cross out the present tense verb in each of the sentences below. Write the past tense of the verb above it.

1. The Graber family works together on the farm.

2. The farmers kill the weeds in the fields.

3. Susan helps with the harvest.

4. Susan lives in a big farmhouse.

5. She likes farm life.

Exercise 6—Word Study

In English, most verbs show the past tense with the *-ed* ending. But some verbs have another form for the past tense. For example, the past tense of *see* is *saw*. The past tense of *come* is *came*.

With your class, write the past tense of the verbs below. These verbs are in the past tense in the next chapter.

Present Tense	Past Tense		Present Tense	Past Tense
1. write	_____		6. make	_____
2. meet	_____		7. go	_____
3. give	_____		8. hear	_____
4. have	_____		9. do	_____
5. tell	_____		10. sit	_____

READING HELPERS

In the LET'S GO section of each chapter, the authors have given you **questions.** The authors say, "Think about the answers to these questions when you read." The questions get your mind ready for reading. They tell you what to look for when you read. They tell you what is important in the reading. The questions are your reasons for reading.

When you read other books, you will not always find questions before each reading. However, it is very important to have some questions in your mind when you are reading. You have to think of your own questions. How can you think of questions? Look at the title of the reading. Look at the pictures and captions. In this way, you can know what the reading is about. Think of what you know about this subject. Think of what you want to find out when you read. These ideas become your questions.

You need practice in thinking of questions before you read. For this reason, in the next three chapters the authors start the questions for you. In the last chapter, the authors give you another way to think of questions.

Questions help you to read well. They give you a reason for reading. They help you find the important information in a reading. Think of questions about the subject before you read.

MORE READING

Supplemental Reading 10—"Americans on the Move"
Supplemental Reading 11—"Raising Sheep"

Chapter 6
Going West

GETTING IDEAS

1. What can you see in this picture?
2. What are these people doing?
3. When was this picture taken?
4. What do you think of when you see this picture?

BUILDING IDEAS

Do you know about the American West? We can see movies with cowboys and Indians. These are about the West, but they are not about the real West. They are fiction. What do we know about the real West? Why did people go west?

the West

problems going west

GETTING READY TO READ

Exercise 1

Read each sentence and talk about the information in it with your class.

1. I am going to move to a new place in the West.
2. There is not much space in the wagon.
3. It was a wide river, but there were rafts for the wagons. Towboats pulled the rafts across the river, but the animals had to swim.
4. We are always sleepy after dinner, so we go to bed as soon as it is dark outside.
5. We are near the foothills of the Wasatch Mountains.
6. We have only some coffee, flour, rice, and dried meat for food.
7. It was 3:00 on Christmas morning when we reached the water and camp.

Exercise 2

Sometimes the information in sentences and your knowledge of the subject can help you understand the meaning of a word. Look at the example below:

> I am going to start a new **diary.** I am going to write in it every day. I will write about all the things I do. When I am old, I can read it again and remember this trip.

What is a *diary?* From the sentences you know it is something to write in. You can write in it every day. It is also something you can read. You can guess that a diary is a kind of book. It is a record about a person's daily life.

Now, read each sentence. Work with a partner. Can you guess the meaning of the word in boldface? When you finish the exercise, use your dictionary to check the meaning of the words.

1. Columbus just came into my bedroom. He is carrying a large book of maps under his arm. He opens the **atlas** and we look at the maps. Columbus wants to find a map of the West.
   What is an **atlas?**

   _____

2. Now we are in a wide open place. There are no trees and no mountains. The land is very flat, and there is tall grass all around. When the wind blows across the **plains,** the grass moves. It looks like a sea of grass.
   What are the **plains?**

   _____

3. The wagon is always moving. It is difficult to ride in it. It goes over rocks. The way is not smooth like a road. It is too **rough** to write. My pen jumps all over the page with every letter.
   What does **rough** mean?

   _____

4. Some people in the wagon train are sick. They have **cholera.** This is a very bad disease. Two men died last week of cholera.
   What is **cholera?**

   _____

Exercise 3

Match the general word with the set of words that are examples of it.

1.	_____ animals	a.	east, north, west
2.	_____ weather	b.	mountain, river, desert
3.	_____ family	c.	horses, oxen, buffaloes
4.	_____ directions	d.	Illinois, Utah, California
5.	_____ states	e.	wind, snow, rain
6.	_____ geography	f.	Easter, Thanksgiving, Christmas
7.	_____ feelings	g.	son, husband, wife
8.	_____ holidays	h.	love, hate, worry

Exercise 4

Look at this map of the United States in 1849. Compare this with a present-day map of the United States. What is different in 1849 from the United States today? Look at the route that Julia and her family followed. Answer these questions:

1. Where is Galesburg?

_____

2. What river must they cross to get to Missouri?

_____

3. What river do they follow after they leave Independence, Missouri?

_____

4. Where do they cross the Rocky Mountains?

_____

5. Where is Death Valley?

_____

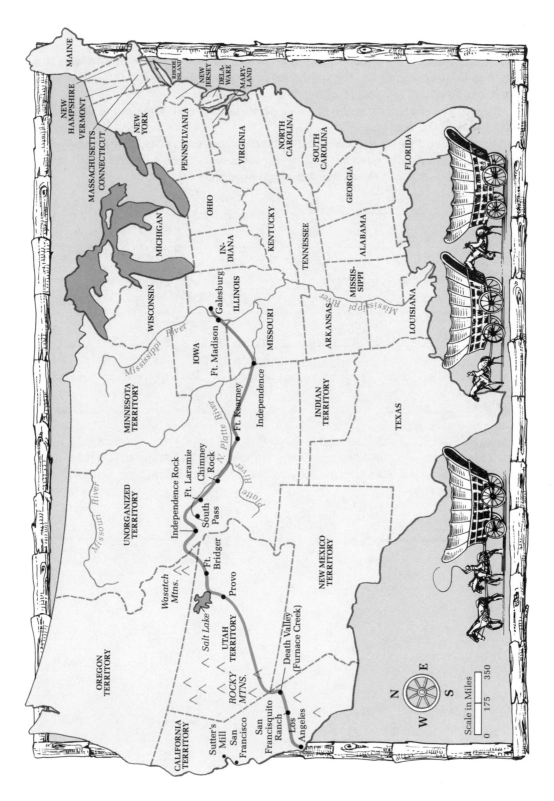

LET'S GO

This reading is part of a diary. Julia Brier wrote in it every day. She moved from Illinois to California in 1849. She went west by wagon train. The trip to California was very hard. The diary is a record of her trip.

Before you read, look at the diary. Look at the pictures. Look at the dates. Get a general idea of the reading.

What do you think the diary will tell us? What questions do you have about Julia's trip west? Write a question that begins with each of the question words below. As you read, think about the answers to these questions.

1. Where _____?

2. Why _____?

3. When _____?

4. How _____?

5. How long _____?

6. Who _____?

7. What _____?

Because this is a diary, you can read each section and stop. Think about what you just read. Think about what will happen next. Think of new questions as you read.

Julia Brier was a real person. As you read, try to imagine how she felt as she moved to California.

——————————— Are you ready to read? ———————————

Julia Brier: A Pioneer Going West

March 24, 1849
Galesburg, Illinois

This is a wonderful day. I am starting a new diary because I am starting an adventure. I am going to move to a new place in the West.

My three boys and I were eating our eggs at the breakfast table this morning. Suddenly, my husband, Mr. Brier, came into the room. He was happy. He said, "A group of local men are planning to go to California. They are going by wagon train. They have about a dozen new covered wagons, horses, and oxen ready to go. They asked me to come along. They need a minister. What do you think?"

The boys shouted, "Yes, let's go!"

I was silent. I looked around my house. I saw all the things I loved. I saw my furniture and books. I can't take all these with me. There is not much space in the wagon. It is difficult to leave these things. I don't want to leave my lovely home, and I don't want to leave my friends. But many people are moving to California. New towns are starting. They need ministers, and my husband wants to go.

"Yes, I will go," I told my husband.

Columbus, my oldest son, just came into my room. He is carrying a large book of maps under his arm. He opens the atlas. He wants to find a maps of the West. Columbus and I look at the map of Illinois. We can see our town, Galesburg. We look at the maps of the West. We can see the Mississippi River. We are going to cross this river. We can see the Platte River. We are going to follow this river. We are going to go through new territories. We will cross the Indians' land into California. The trip is very long. It is about 2,000 miles.

I look out the window at my garden. I see my lovely flowers. This is a beautiful place, and I love my house and home. I am sad to leave this place.

April 13, 1849
Independence, Missouri

We crossed the Mississippi River at Fort Madison on April 4th, three days after we left Galesburg. It is a wide river, but there were rafts for the wagons. Towboats pulled the rafts across the river, but the animals had to swim.

My three boys like the trip. It is an adventure. The covered wagon is not comfortable. It is a rough ride because the ground is not smooth. Usually the boys walk near the wagon. Sometimes they ride on top of one of the horses.

Independence is very busy because there are thousands of people moving west. This is the last city in the United States. Beyond this is the West.

April 20, 1849

We are following the North Platte River. It is very wide, but it is not too deep. I was thankful that the water did not get inside the wagon when we crossed. Some wagons tipped over and everything got wet.

The weather is good. The sky is blue, and the sun is shining. However, April is a rainy month. Rain is not good for us because it makes the ground muddy. The wagons cannot go through the mud. Also, the lightning storms are very bad. Sometimes a tornado comes out of the sky. The high winds of a tornado can break the wagon easily. When it is windy, the wagons cannot move easily.

April 30, 1849

We are traveling slowly. One month ago we left our home in Illinois. Columbus looks at the map and sees that we have a long way to go. We are all good travelers. However, some people in the wagon train are sick. They have cholera. This is a very bad disease. Two men died last week of cholera. It is very sad. I want to go to California, but I don't want my children to be sick.

A few days ago we had a tornado. The tops of some of the wagons blew off. It was terrible.

May 10, 1849
South of Fort Kearney

It is ten days since I wrote in my diary. We did not go to Fort Kearney because they have cholera there. The days are usually the same. We walk beside the wagon or ride in it. I don't like riding in the wagon. It is uncomfortable. Every day we stop the wagon train to sleep. The men make the fire and the women cook dinner. The children help wash the dishes. We are always sleepy after dinner so we go to bed as soon as it gets dark.

Some evenings when there is a moon and the weather is good, we sing around the fire. Some of the men play the fiddle or guitar, and we all sing. This life seems to please my family.

May 16, 1849

We travel about 20 miles each day. My husband, Mr. Brier, showed us the map. We have a long way to go. We are going to pass Chimney Rock. Then we will be near Fort Laramie. From there we go to Independence Rock, our landmark for South Pass.

May 24, 1849
Near Independence Rock

We are in Indian country. A week ago we met some Sioux and Crow Indians for the first time. The boys were very interested in them. They were not afraid.

Independence Rock is very large. You can see it for many miles before you get there. It is a landmark for travelers.

Sometimes we see travelers who are going back to the United States. They do not want to continue into this empty country.

May 30, 1849
South Pass

We are near South Pass. Here we cross the Rocky Mountains. This is going to be difficult. We see more people who are going home.

There is some snow on the mountain tops. Someone told us to watch out for Ute and Shoshone Indians here. They are not happy that white people are coming into their country. We stay close to the other wagons.

June 4, 1849
Fort Bridger

We are at a place called Fort Bridger. The army has soldiers here. We will rest here after a long, hard week. This is the first fort that we have visited. It is a safe place for people from the United States. The gates of the high, stone walls stand open. An American flag is flying.

There are two men at the fort who are going back to the states. They will carry letters for 50 cents apiece! We all want to write to our families. We want to tell them we are all right. The men left with a large bag of mail.

July 23, 1849
Provo, Utah Territory

We are just south of Salt Lake City near the foothills of the Wasatch Mountains. We are staying here for two months or more. It is a good place to wait for cool weather. We cannot travel through this part of the country during the summer months because it is a desert. It is a very hot and dry place.

September 26, 1849

Today is my 36th birthday. The boys sang "Happy Birthday" to me and gave me presents. Kirke is four years old. He gave me some watercress, a plant for salads. Columbus is nine years old. He gave me a small basket. "An Indian showed me how to make it from pine needles," he said. John is seven years old. He made me something from wood. My husband gave me fresh carrots, new potatoes, and a piece of buffalo meat. What a wonderful birthday!

October 15, 1849
Provo, Utah Territory

We are ready to leave again. Many people are ready to go west. There are more than 50 wagons! We are traveling again!

October 30, 1849

We are in very dry country. We camp in the sand and and there is no water. We are all thirsty. We don't know where we are. How far must we go?

After dinner, we sat around the fire. Captain Jefferson Hunt is a guide. He went to California before. He wants $10.00 a wagon to guide us to California. It is too much money! Another man, Mr. Smith, has a map. It shows another way to California. It is shorter than Captain Hunt's trail.

Captain Hunt wants to go south, and Mr. Smith wants to go west. Many people want to go with Mr. Smith. Only seven wagons go with Captain Hunt. We will go with Mr. Smith.

November 4, 1849
Somewhere in the Utah Territory

It is dry and rocky here. There are no trees. We are not happy. Captain Hunt left with the seven wagons, and we said good-bye. The next day Mr. Smith ran away with the map. We have to go through the desert without a map. There are 85 people here. We are going to travel together. We are fearful about this trip.

November 17, 1849

Today is a very bad day. We are in Forty-Mile Canyon, and it is too difficult for our animals to pull the wagons. We have to leave the wagons and walk. We have to leave many things behind. We killed three of the weak oxen for meat. We have only some coffee, rice, flour, and dried meat for food. We have to be careful because there is not much food.

November 22, 1849
Thanksgiving Day

This is Thanksgiving Day, and we are thankful to be alive. I cannot think of a real Thanksgiving dinner. It makes me sad. We walked about ten miles yesterday and will rest here a day. We do not have much food, and I worry about tomorrow.

December 10, 1849

Today we saw something terrible. A wide, flat valley is below us. It looks hot and dry and white with salt. Beyond the valley are very high, snowy mountain peaks. How can we cross this place?

December 27, 1849
Furnace Creek, Death Valley

Three days before Christmas we started down to the valley. For 24 hours we had no water. We walked and walked. My husband walked ahead to look for water. I walked with my three boys. Kirke was very weak, so I carried him on my back. At midnight my husband came back. There was water, but we had to walk six more miles! It was 3:00 on Christmas morning when we reached the water and camp. What a wonderful Christmas present: water! I am thankful my family is alive.

January 9, 1850

After 19 days, we are across the valley. Now we must climb these mountains. I am happy to leave this dreadful place. I want to get to California soon.

We climbed up into the mountains and found snow. It was wonderful to eat. Columbus liked it. "It is better than ice cream," he said. He sounds cheerful.

January 27, 1850

Almost every day someone dies. Our group gets smaller and smaller. We didn't know there were so many valleys and low mountains to cross. This land is not flat, and there is not much water.

February 4, 1850

How wonderful! There is a green valley ahead! We are safe! We are going to live!

February 5, 1850
San Francisquito Ranch, California

Last night I heard the sound of cows. There are only 30 people alive now in our group. We are all very thin and look terrible. Before our trip I weighed 115 pounds (52 kilograms). Now I am just 75 pounds (35 kilograms). My husband is even worse. He weighed 175 pounds (79 kilograms) when we left. Now he also weighs 75 pounds. Some Mexican women brought us some cabbages, corn, and oranges. There was some milk for the boys, too. When we are strong again, we will move on to Los Angeles.

March 31, 1850

Today is Easter Sunday. One year ago we planned our trip from Illinois to California. It is over, and we are in Los Angeles now. We are very thankful.

AFTER READING

Exercise 1

Do you remember the two types of questions you can ask? They are yes/no questions and *wh-* questions (information questions). A yes/no question needs an answer of either *yes* or *no*.

Answer these questions below with *yes* or *no*. If you answer *no*, give the correct information.

1. Is Julia from Illinois?

   _____

2. Are the Briers moving to Colorado?

   _____

3. Do the boys want to go to California?

   _____

4. Is Mr. Brier a banker?

   _____

5. Does Julia have three sons?

   _____

6. Can Julia take her furniture and books with her?

   _____

7. Does the wagon train cross the Mississippi River?

   _____

8. Does Julia like her home in Illinois?

   _____

9. Does the wagon train move quickly?

   _____

10. Is the desert hot in August?

_____

11. Do the Briers get to California?

_____

Exercise 2

Wh- questions do not need the answers *yes* or *no.* These questions need information as the answer.

    Answer the questions with the correct information.

1. When do the Briers leave for California?

_____

2. Where do they stop for the summer months?

_____

3. Why do they leave their wagons?

_____

4. How many wagons go with Captain Hunt?

_____

5. Who is writing the diary?

_____

6. What are some weather problems they have?

_____

7. What was their Christmas present?

_____

8. How many people reach California?

_____

Chapter 6

Do you remember about definitions? If you don't, review the READING HELPERS section in Chapter 4. Now, look back at the reading and find the definitions for these words. The dates can help you find the words quickly in the reading.

1. What is a tornado? (April 20)

_____

2. What is cholera? (April 30)

_____

3. What is a fiddle? (May 10)

_____

4. What is a fort? (June 4)

_____

5. What is a desert? (July 23)

_____

6. What is watercress? (September 26)

_____

Imagine you are a newspaper reporter. You have to write a story about Julia Brier and her family, but the story must be short. Remember, it is a newspaper story. What facts are important for you to tell the reader?

_____

_____

_____

_____

Working with a partner, write a short newspaper story about Julia Brier.

Exercise 5

Julia Brier's diary is a record of a long, hard trip. The reader cannot remember every day of her trip. Below is a chart with some places and dates from the diary. Find the places on the map and write the date by the place. Then, look back at the diary. What happened at or near these places? Complete the chart by writing down some facts you want to remember.

DATE	PLACE	FACTS TO REMEMBER
March 24, 1849	Galesburg, Illinois	
April 4	Fort Madison	
April 13	Independence, Missouri	
May 10	near Fort Kearney	
May 24	near Independence Rock	
May 30	near South Pass	
June 4	Fort Bridger	
July 23	Provo	
November 4	Somewhere in Utah Territory	
December 25	Furnace Creek, Death Valley	
February 5, 1850	San Francisquito Ranch	

Chapter 6

Look at these words:

wonderful	beautiful	careful	dreadful
cheerful	thankful		fearful

They all end with the suffix *-ful.*
    Look at this sentence. *The glass is full of water.*
    This sentence has the word *full* in it. The word means that the glass has water in it. It has water up to its top. It has a lot of water in it. The ending *-ful* has a similar meaning.

The flowers are **beautiful.**

The word *beautiful* means the flowers have a lot of beauty in them. The flowers are "full of beauty." These words are adjectives.

    In the sentences below, make an adjective ending with *-ful* from the noun in parentheses ( ).

1. (pain) Her broken leg was very _____, so the doctor gave her some medicine to stop the pain.

2. (thank) The car did not hit the little girl. Her parents were very _____.

3. (care) The street is very dangerous. The cars go very fast. You must be

    _____ when you cross it.

4. (success) The student studied very hard. He got all A grades. He was

    _____ in his studies.

5. (wonder) This is a _____ day. We are moving to California.

6. (fear) We must go through the desert without a map. I am _____ about this trip.

7. (dread) I am happy to leave this _____ place. It is so horrible.

Another adjective ending is *-y.* Many times we can find this ending when we are talking about the weather.

It is a **rainy** day. This tells us that it is raining outside.
It is a **cloudy** day. This tell us that there are many clouds in the sky.
The water in the river is **muddy.** This tells us that the water is not clean because there is a lot of mud in it.

Can you complete these sentences?

1. There is a lot of snow falling. It is a _____ day.

2. The wind is blowing. It is a _____ day.

3. There are many rocks on the road. It is a _____ road.

4. The sun is shining today. It is a _____ day.

5. There is a lot of dirt in this room. It is a _____ room.

READING HELPERS

Every time you begin to read, you should look quickly through the reading. You know that the title can help you. By looking at the pictures and reading the captions, you can prepare yourself for the reading. When you look at the reading "Julia Brier: A Pioneer Going West," you immediately see that something is different. The reading is divided into small parts, and each part starts with a date. You can guess that this reading is from a diary. You also know that the reading is arranged in a time order. Knowing this can help you when you read. You can always ask yourself, "What will happen next?"

Before the reading you can see a map. You can find Julia Brier's route from Illinois to California on the map. So, before you read, you know that you are going to read a diary, you know that it is about a woman named Julia Brier, and you know she is going west. You also know that she is going from Illinois to California. By using all this information, you can guess that her diary is about her trip. So, you know a lot of information before you read. When you read you can get the details of her trip.

One of the biggest helpers in reading is getting yourself ready to read.

MORE READING

Supplemental Reading 12—"A Letter to Julia"
Supplemental Reading 13—"Death Valley"
Supplemental Reading 14—"The California Gold Rush"

Chapter 7
Celebrating Thanksgiving

GETTING IDEAS

1. Who are the people in each picture?
2. What are the people doing in each picture?
3. How do these people feel?
4. How are these people celebrating Thanksgiving?

BUILDING IDEAS

Do you know about the Thanksgiving holiday? We are going to build ideas about this holiday. You might want to read Supplemental Reading 15 on page 167 before you continue. It is about Thanksgiving.

Thanksgiving Day

Holidays are not always fun for poor people. What are some of the problems poor people have? How do they spend their holidays?

problems of poor people

GETTING READY TO READ

Exercise 1

Circle the word that does not belong in the group.

1. poor	hungry	homeless	happy
2. stranger	family	friends	relatives
3. table	car	chair	bed
4. avenue	street	taxi	road
5. Thursday	Thanksgiving	Christmas	Easter
6. hear	study	see	smell
7. piano	candy	guitar	violin
8. Christian	Moslem	Vietnamese	Jewish
9. coal	oil	wood	water
10. turkey	beans	beef	chicken

Exercise 2

Use your knowledge of the subject and words from the sentences to understand the meaning of each word in boldface.

1. He is an old man. He can't walk very well. He walks slowly and uses a wooden **cane** to help himself.
   What is a **cane**? Can you draw a picture of one?

   _____

2. We didn't have enough money to buy a new car, so we got a **used** car. It is only two years old. The first owner took good care of it, so the car is like new.
   What is a **used** car?

   _____

3. Their new house was empty. They didn't have any chairs or tables. There was no sofa and no bed. "We need to buy some **furniture** soon," said Mary.
   What is **furniture**?

   _____

4. Before the American Civil War (1861–1865), many blacks in the United States were **slaves.** They were not free. They belonged to white people in the South. They worked hard, but they did not get paid.
   What is a **slave**?

   _____

Exercise 3

Read each sentence and talk about the information in it with your class.

1. In a few hours, more than 50,000 people will come to Bruce Randolph Avenue to eat a free Thanksgiving meal of barbecued ribs, turkey, noodles, beans, and coleslaw.
2. These people do not have enough money to fix a big meal at home.
3. Daddy Bruce Randolph is the man who is responsible for this huge Thanksgiving meal. This meal for thousands is his idea.
4. Daddy Bruce's business is selling food.
5. On Thanksgiving morning, we drove a truck full of barbecued ribs over to City Park.
6. This year Daddy Bruce expects to serve turkey to about 100,000 people.
7. The people of Denver admire Daddy Bruce because he gives so much away.
8. Daddy Bruce's grandmother was a slave before the American Civil War.
9. He laughs when he remembers the piano player in his first restaurant.
10. Young people think that Daddy Bruce is a good example to them.

LET'S GO

Look at the title, pictures, and captions in the reading. What do you think it's going to be about? Write a question for each question word below. As you read, think about the answers to these questions.

1. Who _____

2. Where _____

3. What _____

4. How many _____

5. When _____

6. Why _____

———————————— Are you ready to read? ————————————

Thanksgiving Dinner with Daddy Bruce

It's 8 o'clock on a Thursday morning in Denver, Colorado. Usually the streets are busy at this time, but today the streets are unusually quiet. People are not driving to work because it's a holiday. It is Thanksgiving Day. Most people are at home preparing a turkey with dressing, sweet potatoes, cranberry sauce, and pumpkin pie for their Thanksgiving meal. They will eat this holiday meal with their families.

Bruce Randolph Avenue, however, is not a quiet street on this day. Something unusual is happening here. The street's busy, but not with the usual early morning traffic. There are not many cars, but there are hundreds of tables, chairs, and people in the middle of the street. The smell of meat cooking over wood coals fills the air. Everyone's busy. They're cooking food, putting up tables and chairs, and carrying large pots of food. There are about 2,500 people here. They're working, but they will not earn money. They're working because they want to help. In a few hours, thousands of people will come here to eat a free Thanksgiving meal of barbecued ribs, turkey, noodles, beans, and coleslaw.

Many poor people will come here to eat today. These people do not have enough money to fix a big meal at home. Some of them do not even have a place to live. It's not easy to enjoy a holiday when you're poor. However, here on Bruce Randolph Avenue they can eat their Thanksgiving meal for free. They can enjoy their holiday.

"Daddy Bruce," calls a young man, "where should I put these turkey wings?"

"Take them over to that table at the west end of the street," answers an old man who is sitting near the door of a restaurant. The man is Bruce Randolph. Most people call him Daddy Bruce. He is 87 years old. He does not look so old. When he gets up, he walks slowly. He uses a cane to help him walk. But his voice is deep and strong, and the people here listen when he talks. He's responsible for this huge Thanksgiving Day meal. This meal for thousands is his idea.

Daddy Bruce started his Denver restaurant in 1962.

Daddy Bruce owns two buildings on this street. On one corner is Daddy Bruce's Bar-B-Que. This is his restaurant. On the other corner is Daddy Bruce's Bakery and Pizzeria. This is another restaurant. Daddy Bruce's business is selling food, but every Thanksgiving he gives food away. Daddy Bruce began to do this over 20 years ago.

"We started back in 1964," Daddy Bruce explains. "On Thanksgiving morning, we drove a truck full of barbecued ribs over to City Park. We served about 60 people who didn't have a holiday meal."

The newspapers and television stations heard about the free meal and reported it. The next year more poor people knew about the free Thanksgiving meal. Every year the number of people is larger. This year Daddy Bruce expects to serve food to about 100,000 people. Other people who are sick or cannot come to the dinner call Daddy Bruce's restaurant. He sends them a meal. A taxi driver takes the free meal to the person's house.

Food is not the only thing that Daddy Bruce gives away, and Thanksgiving is not the only time he gives. He serves free meals at Christmas and Easter, too, and he has a big party on his birthday. Behind his restaurant is a building full of used furniture and clothing. People who do not need these things any longer bring them to Daddy Bruce. He gives them to people who need them.

"A man called me a few weeks ago. He had a truck full of rice to give me," says Daddy Bruce. "So now when people call me because they don't have anything in the house to eat, I send them over a meal and some of this rice." People call him often. They know he will help them.

Many people admire Daddy Bruce because he gives so much away. It's clear from the smile on his face that Daddy Bruce enjoys giving. His mother often said to him, "You would give away the shirt off your back." He says, "My mother was right. I always believe in trying to help some-body. I love people. I love doing this."

Maybe Daddy Bruce learned about giving from his grandmother. He lived with her in Arkansas when he was a boy. His grandmother was a slave before the American Civil War in the 1860s. She often told Daddy Bruce stories about slavery. He remembers his grandmother: "She always had it good because she was one of the best cooks. She cooked for her master. But she often gave food to hungry people."

Maybe Daddy Bruce learned to cook from his grandmother, too. He opened his first restaurant in Arkansas in 1928. He bought a pig for about five dollars. Then he barbecued it and sold sandwiches for ten cents. He had a piano in his restaurant. People came to eat and dance, and they came to buy candy and cigarettes. He laughs when he remembers the piano player in his first restaurant: "I paid an old guy to play the piano. He only knew one or two songs. He just sat there all night, playing the same song again and again."

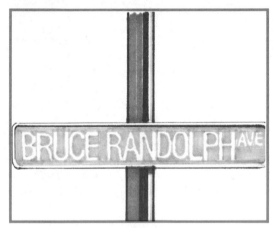

East 34th Street changed to Bruce Randolph Avenue on November 27, 1985.

Daddy Bruce moved to Denver and started his restaurant in 1962. At that time, the street's name was East 34th Street. The restaurant was very successful. It's successful today, too. Many people like to eat there. However, Daddy Bruce does not spend his money like many rich people. "I have a nice car. Since the 1930s I've always had a nice car. A lot of people think I live in a big, fancy house, but I live in the apartment above the restaurant. I have one room with a TV and a bed. I'm happy with it."

Daddy Bruce is a religious man. He does not think that giving is something he learned from his grandmother. He says, "You see, what I do is just a gift from God. He gave us all something to do in life. That's what He gave me—the gift of helping people."

The people of Denver admire Daddy Bruce. The poor people are thankful to him for the food and the clothing. Young people think he is a good example to them. People think that he does a lot of good things for the people of Denver. For these reasons, the city of Denver renamed East 34th Street. They named it Bruce Randolph Avenue. Because of Bruce Randolph, many people in Denver have more to be thankful for on Thanksgiving Day.

AFTER READING

Exercise 1

Write T if the sentence is true (right) and F if the sentence is false (wrong). If the sentence is false, rewrite it with the correct information.

_____ 1. Most of the streets of Denver are quiet because most people are at home.

_____

_____ 2. It's the day before Thanksgiving.

_____

_____ 3. Bruce Randolph Avenue is busy.

_____

_____ 4. Many people will come to Bruce Randolph Avenue to eat a free Thanksgiving meal.

_____

_____ 5. Daddy Bruce's family name is Randolph.

_____

_____ 6. Food's the only thing Daddy Bruce gives away.

_____

_____ 7. Daddy Bruce is a rich man, so he lives in a big, beautiful house.

_____

_____ 8. Daddy Bruce started his first restaurant in 1962.

_____

_____ 9. Daddy Bruce's grandmother was a slave.

_____

_____ 10. Daddy Bruce only helped people after he became successful.

_____

Exercise 2

Complete the sentences with the correct information.

1. Daddy Bruce's first free Thanksgiving meal was in _____ (year) in Denver's City Park.

2. Many people learned about the free Thanksgiving meals from _____

   and _____ .

3. When people cannot come to the Thanksgiving meal, a _____ takes free meals to their houses.

4. When people do not have enough food to eat, they can _____ .

5. The new name for West 34th Avenue is _____

   _____ .

Exercise 3

Look back in the reading, find each boldfaced word, and explain its meaning by using the information in the sentences.

1. In paragraph 2, what are **pots**?

   _____

2. In paragraph 5, can you think of another word for **huge**?

   _____

3. In paragraph 7, what does **served** mean?

   _____

4. In paragraph 8, what does it mean to **report** something?

   _____

5. In paragraph 11, what does **admire** mean? Who are some people you admire?

   _____

6. In paragraph 13, what is another word for **guy**?

_____

7. In paragraph 14, what does a **fancy house** look like?

_____

Exercise 4

We can remember facts about the reading by organizing the things we remember. Can you remember some ways Daddy Bruce helps people? Give some examples:

_____

_____

_____

Why was a street named after Daddy Bruce? Give some reasons:

_____

_____

_____

What other facts from the reading do you think are important to remember about Daddy Bruce? Make a list of your ideas:

_____

_____

_____

_____

Share your list with the other students in your class. What ideas did you all write down? Talk about these ideas with the other students and your teacher. How could you organize these ideas to make it easy to remember the information?

Exercise 5—Word Study

Do you remember the -er, -or, -ist, and -y endings? Those are **suffixes** and go at the end of the word.

Re- is a **prefix** and goes at the beginning of a verb. Look at these words and their meanings:

reread	to read again
rewrite	to write again
review	to look at again
return	to come back (or bring back) to a place again
rename	to name again

Each word begins with re-, and each word has the meaning *again.*

Can you complete each of these sentences with one of the words beginning with re-?

1. You wrote a paragraph. Your teacher wants you to write it again. Your teacher

   wants you to _____ the paragraph.

2. You miss your country very much. You want to go back to see your family. You

   would like to _____ to your country.

3. The people will _____ the street because they admire Daddy Bruce, and want to name the street again.

4. You read a story. You want to read it again because you didn't understand it. You

   want to _____ the story.

5. You are going to have a test on Chapter 3. You want to look at Chapter 3 again.

   You want to _____ the chapter.

Exercise 6—Word Study

Can you define the following boldfaced words?

1. My glass is empty. Would you please **refill** it?

   refill = _____

2. That is my favorite song on the tape. Would you please **replay** it?

    replay = _____

3. Your homework isn't correct. Would you please **redo** it?

    redo = _____

4. The engine in my car is no good. I need to **rebuild** it.

    rebuild = _____

5. Don't throw away that bottle. I can **reuse** it.

    reuse = _____

READING HELPERS

The **main idea** of a paragraph is the most important idea in the paragraph. Often there is one sentence that tells the main idea of the paragraph. The other sentences in the paragraph give more information about the main-idea sentence. The other sentences show the reader that the main idea is true. Sometimes the other sentences are examples of the main idea. Read this example paragraph:

> **Food is not the only thing that Daddy Bruce gives away, and Thanksgiving is not the only time he gives.** He serves free meals at Christmas and Easter, too, and he has a big party on his birthday. Behind his restaurant is a building full of used furniture and clothing. People who do not need these things any longer bring them to Daddy Bruce. He gives them to people who need them.

The first sentence is the main idea. The other sentences are examples of other things and other times that Daddy Bruce gives.

Here is another example paragraph:

> **Spring is a busy time for all Illinois farmers.** In April, the spring planting begins. The farmers plant the corn first. Three or four weeks later, they plant soybeans. When the seeds begin to grow, the farmers put chemical fertilizers on the soil. When the plants are young, the farmers must kill the weeds in the fields. They use chemicals and machines to kill the weeds. Cecil and Susan's father work in the fields from sunrise to sunset.

The first sentence is the main idea. The other sentences give examples of the work that farmers do in the spring. These sentences show that Illinois farmers are busy in the spring.

The main-idea sentence is not always at the beginning of the paragraph. Some-times it comes at the middle or at the end. Read this paragraph:

"A man called me a few weeks ago. He had a truck full of rice to give me," says Daddy Bruce. "So now when people call me because they don't have anything in the house to eat, I send them over a meal and some of this rice." People call him often. **They know he will help them.**

In this paragraph, the main-idea sentence is the last sentence. The main idea of this paragraph is that poor people know Daddy Bruce will help them. In the quotation Daddy Bruce gives an example of what he does to help people.

Sometimes the writer does not put the main idea into one sentence. The reader must ask himself, "What is the writer's main idea?" The reader sees that all of the sentences in the paragraph are about one subject. Read this example:

In the middle of summer, many farmers have time to relax. The crops are growing. However, the Grabers also have animals. They need hay to feed the sheep in winter. Hay is dried grass. A machine cuts the grass and ties it together. Later, they store the hay in the barn for the winter. Usually they make hay four or five times in one summer.

The reader cannot find the main idea of this paragraph in one sentence. How-ever, when the reader thinks about the sentences, he can understand this main idea: **The Graber family must also work hard in the summer because they have sheep.**
Finding the main idea of a paragraph helps the reader to understand the impor-tant ideas in a reading.

MORE READING

Supplemental Reading 15—"The Story of Thanksgiving Day"
Supplemental Reading 16—"A Recipe for Barbecued Ribs"

Chapter 8
Telling Stories

GETTING IDEAS

1. What do you see in this picture?
2. What is the adult doing? What are the children doing?
3. What stories do you remember from your childhood?
4. Did you have a favorite storyteller when you were a child?

BUILDING IDEAS

People told stories in the past. People tell stories today. What kinds of stories are there? What kinds of stories do you like?

$$\boxed{\text{kinds of stories}}$$

Some people tell stories very well. Some people cannot tell an interesting story. Describe a good storyteller. What does a good storyteller do?

$$\boxed{\text{a good storyteller}}$$

GETTING READY TO READ

Exercise 1

Here is more practice with the past tense forms of verbs. Write the correct past tense form in the blank. Choose verbs from the list at the end of the exercise.

Present Tense Form	**Past Tense Form**
1. is	_____
2. are	_____
3. can	_____
4. find	_____
5. write	_____
6. move	_____
7. tell	_____
8. want	_____
9. come	_____
10. feel	_____
11. get	_____
12. leave	_____
13. grow	_____
14. begin	_____
15. think	_____

began	was	told	wanted	found
were	came	got	left	thought
felt	moved	could	wrote	grew

Exercise 2

This reading is about a man from the state of New Mexico. The state of New Mexico has an unusual population. Study the chart below. Then talk with your classmates about this question: What is unusual about the population of New Mexico?

Three Cultural Groups of the United States and New Mexico

| UNITED STATES | NEW MEXICO |

- 100%
- 90%
- 80%
- 70%
- 60%
- 50%
- 40%
- 30%
- 20%
- 10%

United States: **75%** (Anglo), **7%** (Hispanic), **0.68%** (Native American)

New Mexico: **40%** (Anglo), **37%** (Hispanic), **8%** (Native American)

☐ Anglo Population   ▧ Hispanic Population   ■ Native American Population

Exercise 3

Read each sentence and talk about the information in it with your class.

1. Joe Hayes' voice rises and falls.
2. He tells his stories at the Wheelwright Museum of the American Indian in the summer.
3. During the rest of the year, he travels to schools and tells stories to the children there.
4. About 50 years ago, anthropologists, or people who study cultures, wrote down some of the stories of the Native American and Hispanic cultures.
5. When Joe's father told stories about Ireland, he often used an Irish accent.
6. TV uses fast action, lots of pictures, music, and special effects.
7. People had to give all their knowledge about the world to the next generation, so they told stories to pass on their knowledge.
8. Stories get children interested in reading and learning.

LET'S GO

Look at the title of the reading. Look at the pictures in the reading and read the captions by the pictures. What do you think the reading is about?

Write a question that begins with each of the question words below. Write questions that you want to answer when you read. As you read, think about the answers to these questions.

1. Where _____?

2. What kind _____?

3. Who _____?

4. How _____?

5. Why _____?

—————————— Are you ready to read? ——————————

Joe Hayes: A Storyteller

On a summer evening in Santa Fe, New Mexico, you can join a circle of families. The families are sitting among the trees on the side of a hill. One man is speaking. The people, adults and children of all ages, are listening to the man. He stands in front of an Indian tent, or teepee. His voice rises and falls. One minute his voice sounds like the voice of an old woman. The next minute he is talking like an old man, and then he crows like a rooster. The audience listens. Sometimes they laugh. Sometimes they say part of the story with him or move their arms and hands in the same way he does.

The place is the Wheelwright Museum of the American Indian in Santa Fe, New Mexico. The man is Joe Hayes. He is a storyteller. He tells his stories at the museum in the summer. During the rest of the year, he travels to schools and tells stories to the children there. He also talks with teachers about the importance of storytelling. Some of his stories are in children's books and on cassette tapes.

Some of Joe Hayes' stories come from his imagination. These stories are new. However, many of the stories are old stories. Many generations of people have told these stories to their children. These old stories are called folktales.

In New Mexico, where Joe Hayes lives, there are two very interesting groups of people. One group is American Indians. They often call themselves Native Americans because they were the first people who lived in America. The other group is Hispanic Americans. These Americans have lived in this part of the country for many generations. Their first language is Spanish. Most Hispanic Americans are bilingual. They speak Spanish and English.

Joe Hayes wanted to use stories about people who lived in New Mexico. There are folktales from cultures all over the world, but he wanted to use the folktales from the Native American and Hispanic people who live in his part of the world.

Folktales are very old. In the past, the stories were very important in all cultures. However, when Joe Hayes began to look for stories to tell, he could not find people who knew the stories well. They said, "Oh, yes, my father told me that story," but they could not tell the story to their children. So Joe Hayes went to libraries. There he found books of old stories. About 50 years ago, anthropologists, people who study cultures, wrote down some of the stories from the Native American and Hispanic cultures.

Joe's father introduced him to the fun of storytelling. Joe's grandparents came from Ireland to the United States. When Joe's father told stories about Ireland, he often spoke with an Irish accent. Joe liked the stories and the sound of the accent. When his father told stories, Joe felt close to his father. He felt his father's love for him when his father told stories.

Many years later, Joe told stories to his own children. When he worked for a time in Spain, he made tapes with stories to send to his children in the United States. Later, he moved back to the United States. He was an English teacher in a high school. Joe's children lived in California for most of the year, but they spent summers with Joe in New Mexico. He told his children stories in the summer. They had the memory of the stories to take with them when they left in the fall. When his children grew up, he began to look for other children to listen to his stories. He began to tell stories to groups of children in schools and libraries.

At first, he worried. He thought, "Today, children watch TV so much. TV uses fast action, lots of pictures, music, and special effects. Will they like my stories? Will they be interested when there is no TV picture?"

But the children were very interested. They loved Joe's stories. More and more people asked him to tell stories. He stopped teaching. Storytelling became a full-time job.

"In the past," says Joe Hayes, "stories were necessary for survival. There were no books. People had to give all their knowledge about the world to the next generation, so they told stories to pass on their knowledge. Today we have books and television. But I think that stories are still very important today."

Most teachers believe that stories are important for young children. They help children to learn new words in their language. Stories get children interested in reading and learning. Stories help children to use their imaginations. When children watch TV, they do not have to think much. When they listen to a story, they must think more. They must picture the story in their minds.

Joe Hayes' stories do all of those things, but there is another good thing about his stories. Many of his stories are bilingual. He often uses Spanish and English in his stories. The stories teach

Joe tells a story to a class of fifth-grade children.

Hispanic children that it is good to speak Spanish. They teach English-speaking children that another language is interesting and fun. They teach all children that it is good to know more than one language. In addition, because the stories come from more than one culture, they teach children about their own cultures and about the cultures of other people.

Joe Hayes likes his work with children. He likes to see the happy faces of the children. He remembers a five-year-old girl who said to him, "Oh, you gave me a dream!" However, Joe likes storytelling at the museum more. He likes to tell his stories there because whole families come to hear him.

"When I tell a story to families," Joe says, "the adults understand some of the humor that children do not understand. The children think it is interesting to see their parents laugh. The parents like to watch their children enjoying the story, too. Older kids might not enjoy the story when they are with other children of the same age because they like to pretend they are very grown up. They don't want others to think they are little children. However, when they are with their families, they can relax and enjoy the story. Families are my favorite audiences.

"Sometimes families tell me that they remember one of my stories very well. Everyone in the family likes the story," Joe says. "Now when they go camping or on a trip, they tell the story to each other. This makes me feel really good. It makes me feel that I am touching other people's lives and enriching them."

AFTER READING

Finding the main idea in a paragraph can help you to understand the important ideas in a reading. In this exercise, you will practice finding the main idea in some of the paragraphs in the reading, "Joe Hayes: A Storyteller." Find these paragraphs in the reading. Find the main-idea sentence in each paragraph. Circle the letter of the sentence that tells the main idea.

1. Paragraph 4:
    a. In New Mexico, where Joe Hayes lives, there are two very interesting groups of people.
    b. They speak Spanish and English.
    c. These Americans have lived in this part of the country for many generations.
2. Paragraph 7:
    a. When Joe's father told stories about Ireland, he often spoke with an Irish accent.
    b. Joe liked the stories and the sound of the accent.
    c. Joe's father introduced him to the fun of storytelling.
3. Paragraph 12:
    a. Stories get children interested in reading and learning.
    b. When children watch TV, they do not have to think much.
    c. Most teachers believe that stories are important for young children.
4. Paragraph 15:
    a. The children think it is interesting to see their parents laugh.
    b. Families are Joe's favorite audiences.
    c. Older kids don't want others to think they are little children.

In some paragraphs, the main idea is not in one sentence. You must ask yourself, "What is the writer's main idea?" Find these paragraphs in the reading. These paragraphs do not have the main idea in one sentence. Below are sentences that describe the main idea of these paragraphs. Circle the letter of the sentence that tells the main idea.

1. Paragraph 8:
    a. Joe's children liked his stories.
    b. Joe lived far from his children.
    c. Joe told stories to his children before he told them to other children.
2. Paragraph 13:
    a. Joe's bilingual stories teach children some important things.
    b. Joe's bilingual stories teach children that it is good to speak Spanish.
    c. Joe's bilingual stories teach children about their own cultures.

3. Paragraph 16:
   a. Families tell Joe's stories on camping trips.
   b. Joe feels good when his stories touch other people's lives.
   c. All the members of the family like his stories.

Exercise 3

Complete the sentences below. Look back in the reading for help. When you complete the sentences, you will know some of the important ideas in the reading.

Joe Hayes is a storyteller. He tells his stories at a _____ in the summer

and at _____ during the rest of the year. Many of his stories are folktales

from the _____ and the _____ who live in

New Mexico. He could not find many people who knew these old stories well, so he

_____. There he found _____.

When Joe was a child, his father _____. When Joe became a

father, he told stories _____. When his children grew up, Joe

_____.

Joe worried that children might not like his stories because

_____. However, the children _____.

Joe is now a full-time _____.

Exercise 4

A reading gives us new ideas. Reading also helps us to think of our own ideas about a subject. Answer these questions with ideas from the reading first. Then think of your own ideas about the questions. Discuss these ideas with your class.

1. Why are stories important for children?

   Ideas from the Reading:

   _____

   _____

   _____

Can you add more reasons?

_____

_____

_____

2. How do Joe's bilingual stories help children?

    Ideas from the Reading:

    _____

    _____

    _____

    Can you add more ways?

    _____

    _____

    _____

3. Why does Joe like his job?

    Ideas from the Reading:

    _____

    _____

    Would you like to be a storyteller?

Exercise 5—Word Study

The word *like* is often a problem for learners of English. We read and hear the word often. *Like* is a problem because it has different meanings. Talk with your classmates about the different meanings in these sentences:

> The children **like** Joe's stories.
> Joe's voice sounds **like** the voice of an old woman.

In the first sentence *like* is a verb. It means "enjoy or think something or someone is good.'' In the second sentence, *like* is used as a preposition and means that Joe's voice and an old woman's voice are the same in many ways.

Do you understand the difference in these sentences?

> The boy likes his father.
> The boy is like his father.

The first sentence is about the boy's feelings for his father. The reader knows that he thinks his father is a good person. The second sentence says that the boy and his father are the same in many ways.

Read the sentences below. When *like* means enjoy or think something is good, write *enjoy* in the blank. When *like* means same, write *same* in the blank.

_____ 1. Most children like to watch TV.

_____ 2. Joe crows like a rooster.

_____ 3. Joe Hayes likes his work with children.

_____ 4. He likes to see the happy faces of the children.

_____ 5. The students like Elizabeth.

_____ 6. Tom Carr looks like Mike Carr.

_____ 7. Like her parents, Susan lives on a farm.

_____ 8. Daddy Bruce likes to give.

_____ 9. Daddy Bruce is like his grandmother.

_____ 10. Julia Brier's sons liked going West.

READING HELPERS

It is important to understand the **order** of what happens in a story. In other words, the reader must understand what happens first, second, third, and so on. Folktales and many other stories often use words that tell about order. Here is a short folktale. The words that show order are in boldface. When you read, look for these words in the story. They will tell you the order of the important things in the story. Talk about the meanings of those words with your class.

The Little Red Hen wanted to plant some wheat. **First,** she asked the Dog, "Will you help me to plant some wheat?"

The Dog said, "I will not."

She asked the Cat **second,** "Will you help me to plant some wheat?"

"I will not," said the Cat.

Third, she asked the Rat, "Will you help me to plant some wheat?"

The Rat answered, "I will not."

So the Little Red Hen said, "I will plant the wheat myself."

After the Little Red Hen planted the wheat, it grew. **When** the wheat was ripe, the Little Red Hen said, "Who will help me cut the wheat?"

Then the Dog, the Cat, and the Rat answered, "We will not."

So the Little Red Hen said, "I will cut the wheat myself."

Later, when the wheat was cut, the Little Red Hen said, "**Before** I can make bread, the miller must grind the wheat into flour. Who will take the wheat to the miller?"

Again the Dog, the Cat, and the Rat answered, "We will not."

So the Little Red Hen said, "I will take it myself."

At last, the Little Red Hen was ready to bake the bread. "Who will help me bake some bread?" she asked.

"We will not," answered the Dog, the Cat, and the Rat together.

So the Little Red Hen said, "I will do it myself."

Next, the Little Red Hen mixed the bread and put it in the oven to bake. **When** the bread was golden brown, she took it from the oven. It smelled delicious. **Soon,** the Dog, the Cat, and the Rat ran to the Little Red Hen. "Who will help me eat the bread?" asked the Little Red Hen.

"We will!" said the Dog, the Cat, and the Rat together.

"Oh, no, you will not," said the Little Red Hen. "I will eat it myself."

Finally, she called her chicks to her and shared the bread with them.

MORE READING

Supplemental Reading 17—"City Mouse and Country Mouse"
Supplemental Reading 18—"The Story of the Sioux Indians of North America"

Chapter 9
Following a Dream

GETTING IDEAS

1. Who are the people in this picture?
2. What are they doing?
3. Where do you think these people live?
4. What is the woman's job?

BUILDING IDEAS

Many children dream of what they will be when they grow up. What are some things a child wants to be? Where does a child get these ideas? How can a person make these dreams come true?

I want to be...

Sometimes a child wants to be a professional singer. What kinds of singing careers are there? What does a singer need to study?

singing career

GETTING READY TO READ

What do you want to be
when you grow up?

Exercise 1

Look at the picture above. This little girl is thinking about her future. She wants to be an astronaut. Some people tell her, "You can't be an astronaut. It's too hard." But she reads a book about a woman who is an astronaut. The little girl wants to be like this woman. This woman is her **role model,** an example of success.

Many people can be role models. We look for some quality in the person and try to be like that person. Each person in this book has a quality that is good to model.

For example, Hue Truong worked very hard to learn English. She wanted to go back to school. She worked very hard to succeed. She is a good example for students.

Why is each person below a good example of a role model? How can each person be a role model? Discuss this with your class.

1. Elizabeth Carr
2. Tom and Mike Carr
3. Dennis Trone
4. Susan Graber
5. Daddy Bruce
6. Julia Brier
7. Joe Hayes

Can you think of other people who can be role models?

Exercise 2

Think about your country and culture. Each situation and question below can be answered differently depending on the culture a person comes from. How does someone from your country and culture answer each question? Write down your answers and compare them with your classmates. Discuss the differences between your answers. Are there differences about time? Are there differences in ways to say "no"? Are there differences in the family?

1. You have a business appointment at 10:00 A.M. When do you arrive for the appointment?

    _____

2. You are invited to a dinner party at a friend's house. It begins at 8:00. What time do you arrive at the house?

    _____

3. You are invited to a friend's house for a party on Saturday night. What time do you arrive at the house?

    _____

4. The bus schedule says the bus will arrive at 3:25 P.M. What time do you get to the bus stop? What time will the bus arrive?

    _____

5. Your teacher asks the class, "Did you understand the homework?" You didn't understand. What do you do?

    _____

6. After a lesson, your teacher asks, "Are there any questions?" You didn't understand the lesson. What do you say?

    _____

7. You are at a friend's house for dinner. You didn't like the food. She asks, "How was the dinner?" What do you say?

    _____

8. You are graduating from school. Your teacher asks, "Please invite your family." What relatives do you invite?

    _____

9. Someone asks you, "How many people are in your family?" What relatives are included in your answer?

    _____

Exercise 3

Read each sentence and talk about the information in it with your class.

1. Bonnie Jo Hunt is a Hunkpapa Lakota Indian from Standing Rock Reservation in South Dakota.
2. Bonnie Jo wants Indians to be proud of their culture and the history of the Indian people.
3. When she was 12, her family moved to Valier, Montana (population 710).
4. After finishing high school, she entered the music department at the University of Montana.
5. She likes foreign languages because she can learn about other cultures.
6. In 1980, Bonnie Jo started her organization, Artists of Indian America.
7. The artists work with the community and school to present a wonderful and entertaining show.
8. Before they go to a reservation or small town, they spend about three months planning the program.

LET'S GO

Look at the reading. Look at the title, pictures, and captions. This reading also has **subtitles.** A subtitle is like a title, but it is only for a part of the reading. It is like a chapter in a book. Longer readings often have subtitles. Subtitles can give us an idea of the important parts of the reading.

What are the subtitles in this reading? Change each subtitle to a question and write each question below.

1. _____

2. _____

3. _____

4. _____

As you read, think about the answers to these questions.

——————————— Are you ready to read? ———————————

Bonnie Jo Hunt: Following a Dream

Bonnie Jo Hunt is a Hunkpapa Lakota Indian from Standing Rock Reservation in South Dakota. She is an opera singer, and she once sang for the president of the United States in the White House. The president was Lyndon Johnson, who served from 1963–1968. Now she lives in Albuquerque, New Mexico. Before this, she lived in Nigeria and Egypt. She is also the president of Artists of Indian America (AIA). She started this organization, and it is very important to her.

Bonnie Jo started AIA because she wanted to work with Indians. She wanted Indians to be proud of their culture and their Indian history. She wanted Indian children to have successful Indian role models. Finally, she wanted to introduce Indian children to the performing arts: music, dance, and drama. AIA visits Indian communities in the United States. The artists work with the community and school to present a wonderful and entertaining show. They want Indian children to work with them on this show. Bonnie Jo wants the students to see that they can be part of this successful show.

A Dream to Be a Singer

When she was a child, Bonnie Jo did not see very much professional singing and dancing. She grew up on Indian reservations and in small, country towns. Live entertainment was unusual because entertainers did not come to these places. When she was six, she first heard a symphony on the radio and really liked the sound of the instruments. When she was ten, she heard opera on the radio. She really liked the sound of the opera singers, too. She decided that she wanted to be an opera singer when she grew up.

It wasn't easy to become an opera singer. First, her father said, "You don't want to be an opera singer. All opera singers are big and fat." Then her grandmother said, "You can never be an opera singer. You don't have a loud voice." Many people said her dream was impossible. "Oh, no," people said to her, "You don't want to be a singer. Indians don't do that." There were no Indian opera singers, so nobody thought it was possible. There were no role models for Bonnie Jo.

Bonnie Jo did not listen to the words, "You can't be an opera singer." She started singing along with the radio. When she was 12, her family moved to Valier, Montana (population 710). She entered singing contests and sang at the community center. There were no music classes in Valier, but Bonnie Jo always found a place to sing. She even sang in her sleep.

Bonnie Jo sings many kinds of songs: opera arias, Broadway musical songs, Indian love songs, and many more.

After high school, Bonnie Jo entered the music department at the University of Montana. Her father wanted her to study business so that she could get a good job after college. He did not think it was a good idea to be a singer. But Bonnie Jo was a good singer. Finally, her father said, "All right, you can study music."

Bonnie Jo always wanted to be an opera singer.

Her music classes were very difficult. Bonnie Jo could sing, but she could not read music. She didn't study music when she was a child. She had a lot to learn. "I always wanted to be an opera singer since the time I was ten, and the hard work at the university didn't stop my dream," Bonnie Jo says.

A Chance to Learn About Other Cultures

After graduating from college, she began to sing with the San Francisco Opera Company. However, this lasted only one year. She married and moved to Nigeria with her husband. Two years later they moved to Cairo, Egypt.

During her years overseas, Bonnie Jo continued to sing and study. She gave many concerts while she lived overseas. She studied music and foreign languages. She can sing in nine languages.

She likes foreign languages because she can learn about other cultures. Many things about the culture in Egypt were like her Indian culture. For example, there were similar ideas about time, politeness, and family.

In the United States, time is very important. In both the Egyptian culture and the Indian culture, time is not always so important. "It is silly to have to rush and push yourself because of a clock. If I had the time I needed, I would often be three hours late," Bonnie Jo says.

In both Egyptian and Indian cultures it is impolite to say the word "no." It is very bad to say something that will hurt another person, and saying "no" may hurt someone. "When an Indian doesn't answer a question, then the answer is no. The Indian does not answer because he does not want to hurt your feelings. Many non-Indians think the answer is yes, but that is not true," says Bonnie Jo. "In Egypt, it is also impolite to say no."

The family is important in all cultures, but the extended family is very important to both Egyptians and Indians. An extended family includes the parents, children, aunts, uncles, cousins, grandparents, and other relatives. "We have huge audiences for our AIA concerts," Bonnie Jo says. "We visited a little town called Thoreau. Its population is 950 people. But every year there are over 1,500 people at our concerts because the aunts, uncles, and grandparents come. The whole family comes. Indians think that the poorest person in the world is the person without a family," says Bonnie Jo.

A New Direction

After six years in Egypt, Bonnie Jo and her husband returned to the United States for one year. It was 1976, and they returned for the 200th birthday of the United States of America. Bonnie Jo put together a show. "I made this program for people in small towns because I grew up in small towns. Nobody cares about small towns. We never had live entertainment," Bonnie Jo explains.

Bonnie Jo traveled all over the United States. Many times school principals asked her to come to their school. They wanted her to talk to their students. They wanted her to be a role model for the students. "We want you to talk about your Indian heritage for our students," they said to her. Bonnie Jo went to the schools. She talked about her own challenges. She talked about her dream to be an opera singer. She sang for the students. "Before, I never sang opera for Indian people," Bonnie Jo says. "I didn't think they would like it. I was wrong. They were very proud that an Indian person was an opera singer." She told the students, "If I can be an opera singer, you can be anything you want to be."

Indian children from Jemez Pueblo perform a dance.

Bonnie Jo returned to Egypt for two more years, but she always thought about these students. She didn't want to go back to the United States and be an opera singer in a big city. Bonnie Jo wanted to sing for the Indian children. Her dream was moving in a new direction.

Artists of Indian America

In 1980, Bonnie Jo Hunt started her organization, AIA. Now she has about 20 people working with her. People hear about AIA from other people. "We don't do any advertising," Bonnie Jo says. "It is all done by word of mouth. People hear about us, and I send them more information. People invite us because they want the school children to have positive role models."

Planning a show is not easy. Bonnie Jo and the other artists in AIA do not go to a community just to give a concert. They go there for a week to work with the students. Before they go to a reservation or small town, they spend about three months planning the program. They must do many things. For example, the people at the school have to plan some parts of the show. Maybe some students will do a traditional Indian dance. Maybe they will sing a song. A person in the town has to do this planning. This person is the coordinator. In Albuquerque, Bonnie Jo and her artists also plan some acts. For example, Bonnie Jo will sing from some operas. George Flying Eagle, one of the artists, may play the flute, or he may do an Indian hoop dance. There are also some acts that the students and the artists do together. For three months, Bonnie Jo is busy writing letters and talking on the telephone. She talks with the coordinator many times. After all the planning, the people from AIA go out to the community.

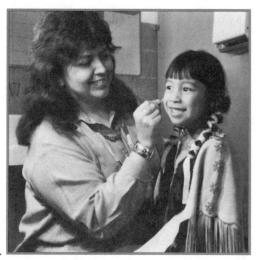

A girl gets ready for a performance.

The final week is a busy one. On Sunday, Bonnie Jo and the other AIA people arrive and have a meeting with the coordinator. Monday, Tuesday, and Wednesday morning the students and artists practice for the show. Wednesday afternoon is the dress rehearsal, or final practice. Thursday morning is the last chance for changes. Thursday afternoon the students and artists from AIA do the show for the school, and Thursday evening they do it for the community.

However, the work does not stop after the show. Friday morning the students and the people from AIA talk. Now is the time for students to ask questions. Now is the time for Bonnie

Jo and the other artists to tell the students, "You, too, can be a success. You can do whatever you want to do in life, if..."

The "if" is very important. Bonnie Jo explains a way to be successful. First, the students have to decide what they want to do. Next, they must plan a way to get it. Then, they have to look for the opportunities and start working. Finally, the students need to work and work. Bonnie Jo says, "Work your head off and don't be afraid to change your goals. You always need to be flexible."

"You also need to be kind to yourself. Reward yourself for small successes," Bonnie Jo tells students. "When I was in school, I set goals. Maybe I didn't want to be in some class, but I needed the class to finish school. I would set tiny goals: finish that term paper and take that test. Soon I could finish the class and start new goals. My final goal was always to be an opera singer. However, there are always many small goals before you reach your final one."

Bonnie Jo always wanted to be an opera singer. It was her dream. Now she is helping many Indian students to find their dream. She is a good example to them. They can have a dream and make it come true, too.

This is a program from an AIA performance.

AFTER READING

Exercise 1

Answer the questions with short answers.

1. What Indian tribe is Bonnie Jo from?

    _____

2. Where did she grow up?

    _____

3. How many people lived in Valier, Montana?

    _____

4. What did Bonnie Jo study at the University of Montana?

    _____

5. What opera company did she sing for?

    _____

6. Why did she move to Nigeria?

    _____

7. Where did she live after she left Nigeria?

    _____

8. How many foreign languages does Bonnie Jo know?

    _____

9. When did Bonnie Jo start Artists of Indian America?

    _____

10. How long does it take to plan a program for a school?

    _____

Chapter 9

Use information from the reading to complete each list.

1. Name three things that Bonnie Jo wanted AIA to do.

    _____

    _____

    _____

2. Name two things Bonnie Jo heard on the radio as a child.

    _____

    _____

3. Name two states that Bonnie Jo has lived in.

    _____

    _____

4. Name three things that the Egyptians and the Indian people have similar ideas
    about.

    _____

    _____

    _____

5. Name four things a student must do to be successful.

    _____

    _____

    _____

    _____

Exercise 3

Circle the letter of the sentence that describes the main idea of each paragraph from the section called **A Dream to Be a Singer.**

1. Paragraph 1:
   a. Bonnie Jo grew up on reservations and in small, country towns.
   b. She was ten when she first heard opera.
   c. Bonnie Jo likes music.
   d. Bonnie Jo decided she wanted to be an opera singer when she was very young.
2. Paragraph 2:
   a. Her father didn't want her to be an opera singer.
   b. Many people told Bonnie Jo she couldn't be an opera singer.
   c. AIA encourages children to do what they want.
   d. Indians are not opera singers.
3. Paragraph 3:
   a. Bonnie Jo moved to Montana.
   b. Bonnie Jo did not become an opera singer.
   c. Bonnie Jo took every opportunity to sing because she wanted to be a singer.
   d. Bonnie Jo entered singing contests and sang at the community center.
4. Paragraph 4:
   a. Bonnie Jo entered the music department at the University of Montana.
   b. Bonnie Jo's father wanted her to study business.
   c. Bonnie Jo was a good singer.
   d. Bonnie Jo finished high school.

Now, write the main idea of each paragraph in the section **A Chance to Learn About Other Cultures.**

Paragraph 1: _____

Paragraph 2: _____

Paragraph 3: _____

Paragraph 4: _____

Paragraph 5: _____

Paragraph 6: _____

Exercise 4

Imagine you are writing a television news report about Bonnie Jo Hunt. You want to tell people a little about her, and you want to talk about Artists of Indian America.

Work with some of your classmates as a news team. Write a short news report. Remember, news stories are not long. The television station wants your report to be three minutes long.

Exercise 5—Word Study

Sometimes a prefix can have the meaning "not." *He was an unhappy person.* This sentence tells us that this person is **not** happy. The prefix *un-* has the meaning "not."
What is the meaning of each word in boldface below?

1. It is **unusual** to see students in suits in the USA.

   unusual = _____

2. That problem is **unimportant.** Don't worry about it.

   unimportant = _____

3. This disease is **uncommon.** Not very many people have it.

   uncommon = _____

4. He is very **unlucky.** He was in a car accident this morning, and someone robbed his house this afternoon.

   unlucky = _____

5. This hot weather is **uncomfortable.** I don't feel very well.

   uncomfortable = _____

Exercise 6—Word Study

Sometimes the prefixes *in-* or *im-* also mean "not." What do these boldfaced words mean?

1. This is an **inexpensive** car. It doesn't cost a lot of money.

   inexpensive = _____

2. Many people said Bonnie Jo's dream was **impossible.** She could not do it.

   impossible = _____

3. It is **impolite** to say "no" to another person. This might hurt their feelings.

impolite = _____

READING HELPERS

A good reader uses many helpers. This book mentioned some of these reading helpers. Here are some reading helpers to remember:

1. Have a reason for reading. It is difficult to read without a purpose.
2. Preview your reading. Look at the title, pictures, maps, captions, and subtitles to get ideas about the reading. You can also look at the reading quickly for a general idea before you read for details.
3. Have a plan for your reading. What will you do with the information you read about? When you must answer questions after you read, look at the questions before you read. This will give you something to read for. You can also think of questions you want to answer.
4. Don't stop reading every time you do not know a word. You don't have to use the dictionary every time you see a word you do not know. Many times, you can find the meaning (the definition) in the reading. The *be* verb (*is, are, am, was, were*), the word *means*, and commas all are signals of a definition. Also use your knowledge to help you guess at a meaning.
5. Look at punctuation clues. A period means the end of a sentence (and an idea). A comma can mean a definition will follow, or it can join ideas. Quotation marks show us the exact words of a speaker.
6. Look for word clues. Words like *first, then,* and *next* give us information in a time order. Words like *but* and *however* show us a difference. *Because* gives us a reason.
7. Look for the main idea of each paragraph, and try to guess what the next idea will be. You can underline (or highlight) the main idea or make a note in the margin to help you remember.
8. Organize your ideas as you read so that you can remember the information.
9. Try not to read out loud. This can slow you down.
10. Read a lot.

MORE READING

Supplemental Reading 19—"American Indians in the United States"
Supplemental Reading 20—"Bonnie Jo Starts to Sing"

APPENDIX ONE
Supplemental Readings 1–20

Supplemental Reading 1

What's Your Name?

Everything has a name. All people, places, and things have names. For example, Hue Truong is the name of a student from Vietnam. Vietnam is the name of her country. Cities and towns have names, too. Schools and office buildings also have names. All things have names. For example, carrot, potato, and bean are names of vegetables. Apple, orange, and banana are names of fruits. Names are important.

We use names every day. When we meet a new person, we usually ask, "What's your name?" It is important to learn a person's name. Most people have two names. Some people have more names. Names are different all over the world. In Hue's class, Hue must learn the names of students from all over the world. This is very difficult because the names are very different.

In the United States, most people have a first name, a middle name, and a last name. Parents choose the first and middle names for their baby. There are names for boys and names for girls. For example, John, Peter, Tom, and Mike are all names for boys. Elizabeth, Bonnie, Susan, and Mary are all names for girls. The last name is the family name. Usually it is the father's family name. In a family, the mother, father, and children usually have the same last name.

Sometimes a person has a nickname, too. A nickname is a special name. It is not a person's real name. Abraham Lincoln's nickname was "Honest Abe." An honest person always tells the truth, and Abe is short for Abraham. Because Lincoln was an honest person, his nickname was "Honest Abe." Pelé is a nickname, too. The soccer player's real name is Edson Arantes do Nascimento, but everyone calls him Pelé. Do you have a nickname?

Names are different all over the world. They can be long or short, but they are always important.

CHECK YOUR UNDERSTANDING

Answer the questions with short answers.

1. What is your last name?

    _____

2. What is your first name?

    _____

3. What is the name of your school?

    _____

4. What is the name of your country?

    _____

5. What is the name of the president of the United States?

    _____

6. What is the name of the ruler of your country?

    _____

7. What is the name of your favorite singer?

    _____

8. What are the names of three of your classmates?

    _____

    _____

    _____

9. Do you have a nickname? What is it?

    _____

Supplemental Reading 2

Do you remember your first day of school? This is a story about a student. Her name is Maria. It is a story about her first day at an English language school.

Maria Starts School

Today Maria is starting school. It is her first day. She is going to study English. She is a little nervous. She has many questions in her head. "Can I understand the teacher? Can I make friends?" Maria asks herself.

At 9:00 Maria and the other new students go to a big room. The teachers and the director are in the room, and are smiling. They are happy to meet the new students.

The director introduces all the teachers. Next, the students introduce themselves. Then one of the teachers talks about the schedule for the day. Today all the students are going to take a test. It is an English language test.

Maria can understand a little. She looks at the other students. There is a student from China and another from Thailand. There are two students from Ecuador. They are brothers. Maria is from Mexico. Some other students are from Vietnam. Three students are from Japan. There is a student from France and one from Germany. Maria is thinking, "I can learn about many countries and practice my English."

Then the students fill out a registration form. The form asks for their address in the United States, a telephone number, and their address in their home countries. One of the teachers helps Maria with her form.

After this, all the students go on a tour. Some of the teachers show them important places in the building. For example, they show them the bookstore, the cafeteria, and the classrooms.

Now it is time for the test. There are three parts to the test. The first part is a writing test. Maria likes writing, so she is happy. It is easy. The second part of the test is a listening test. This is not easy. The people speak too fast on the tape, so Maria can't understand them. She is nervous. She feels sad.

Some of the test questions are difficult.

After the test, it is time for lunch. All the students go to the cafeteria. They begin to talk to each other. One student says, "Oh, the test is too hard!" Maria says, "Yes, I can't understand anything. The people speak too fast." Other students say the same thing. Then they talk about their homes. They talk about coming to the United States. Some of them speak English very well. Some of them are beginners.

After lunch, they return to finish the test. The last part of the test is a grammar and reading test. Maria works very hard, but she can't understand many questions. She wants to use her dictionary, but she can't because it is a test. "I need to study a lot of English," she thinks.

It is 3:00 in the afternoon, and the test is over. All the students can go home now. Maria is tired. She wants to go home and go to sleep. Tomorrow her classes begin. Tomorrow she starts to learn English.

CHECK YOUR UNDERSTANDING

Circle the letter of the best answer.

1. This is a story about _____.
   a. how to learn English
   b. a language school and its students
   c. the first day of school

2. Maria is from _____.
   a. Ecuador
   b. Mexico
   c. Vietnam

3. There are two students from _____.
   a. Japan
   b. Ecuador
   c. China

4. There are _____ parts to the test.
   a. one
   b. two
   c. three

5. Maria feels _____ after the listening test.
   a. sad
   b. angry
   c. happy

6. The _____ test is easy for Maria.
   a. writing
   b. listening
   c. grammar

7. After the grammar and listening test, _____.
   a. Maria has some coffee
   b. Maria goes home
   c. Maria has lunch

Supplemental Reading 3

Elizabeth Carr was a teacher when she was young. This is a letter from Elizabeth to her parents. Look at the date on the letter. Elizabeth writes this letter when she has her first teaching job. What can you learn about Elizabeth's past? What can you learn about this school in Texas in 1935?

A Letter Home

Burleson, Texas
September 15, 1935

Dear Mother and Dad,

Today I am very happy. I like my teaching job. Sometimes teaching is easy and fun. Sometimes it is difficult. You will understand my feelings because you are teachers, too. Let me write about my day.

Every morning I go to school at 7:30. All the teachers are at the school by 8:00. The school director stands at the door and looks at his watch. He is not happy when someone is late. I go to my classroom. From 8:00 to 9:00 I prepare my lessons.

At 9:00 the big bell on top of the school rings. The children stand in lines outside the school door. They are very quiet. Then the director says, "Come in." They walk into the school. After everyone says the Pledge of Allegiance to the United States flag, the lessons begin.

I teach six classes. Most of my students are in grades 9, 10, and 11. I teach typing, shorthand, business law, bookkeeping, and business arithmetic. I also teach one class of fourth graders. I like the fourth graders very much. They are so little and cute. The big boys in my 11th grade class are sometimes a problem.

My classes are not full. More children are going to come to class next week. They are not in school now. They are working in the cotton fields. Often I play the piano for all the children in the school. They like to sing, and I like to play for them.

At 3:30 the children go home. I work at my desk for half an hour, and at 4:00 I go home to my room at the Parnham family's house.

I will get my first paycheck at the end of the month. I get $82.50 each month for nine months. I am so happy to have a job in these hard times.

I pay the Parnham family $4.00 every week for my room and meals. They are a nice family. My roommate is a teacher at my school, too. I like the Parnhams, but I miss you. I miss Mother's cooking.

On Friday night, I am going to go to the basketball game at the school. Some of my students are going to play. Our team will play the team from Joshua. Everyone in the town will be there.

Do you remember an important day next month? On October 26, I will be 20 years old. Can you come to visit me on that day? Write to me soon. I miss you.

Love,

Elizabeth

CHECK YOUR UNDERSTANDING

Exercise 1

Write T if the sentence is true (right) and F if the sentence is false (wrong). When the sentence is false, rewrite it with the correct information.

_____ 1. Elizabeth's mother and father are teachers.

_____

_____ 2. The children come to school at 8:30.

_____

_____ 3. The children make a lot of noise when they go into the school.

_____

_____ 4. Elizabeth teaches only little children.

_____

_____ 5. Some children are not in school because they are working.

_____

_____ 6. Elizabeth lives alone in an apartment.

_____

_____ 7. Elizabeth is going to stay at home on Friday night.

_____

Exercise 2

Answer the questions with numbers.

1. How many classes does Elizabeth teach?

_____

2. How much money will Elizabeth earn in one year?

_____

3. How much money does Elizabeth pay for her room and meals in one month?

_____

4. How old is Elizabeth when she writes this letter?

_____

5. How old is Elizabeth now?

_____

Supplemental Reading 4

Chapter 2 is about Elizabeth Carr. It is about her job. This reading is about her family.

Elizabeth's Family

Elizabeth Carr is a secretary at a language school in Colorado. She works part-time, and she likes her job. She lives near the school, and she drives to work every day. Elizabeth lives in Denver, Colorado, now, but she is not from Colorado. She is from Texas. Now she is a secretary, but she was a teacher in Texas many years ago.

Elizabeth lives by herself in an apartment. Her husband died in 1974. Elizabeth has two children. They are girls. They do not live with Elizabeth. They are married and live with their husbands. One daughter, Caroline, lives in Colorado Springs. The other daughter, Diane, lives in Iowa. Elizabeth likes to visit her daughters.

Colorado Springs is about 60 miles south of Denver. On weekends Elizabeth drives to Colorado Springs to visit Caroline, Bill, Cliff, and Jessica. Bill is Caroline's husband. Cliff is their son, and Jessica is their daughter. Elizabeth likes to visit her grandchildren. She stays with them Saturday and Sunday. Then she drives back to Denver because she has to work on Monday.

Elizabeth's other daughter lives in Iowa. Her husband's name is Mark. Iowa is not near Colorado. It takes two hours by plane to go to Iowa. Elizabeth visits her daughter every year. Diane and Mark come to Denver, too. When they come to Denver, the whole family can get together.

Elizabeth has a nice family, and she loves her family very much. "Now I am a grandmother for my family and for the students at school," Elizabeth says. "I like that."

CHECK YOUR UNDERSTANDING

Circle the letter of the best answer.

1. Elizabeth is from _____.
   a. Colorado
   b. Texas
   c. Iowa

2. Elizabeth lives in _____.
   a. Colorado
   b. Texas
   c. Iowa

3. Elizabeth has _____.
   a. one son and two daughters
   b. two daughters
   c. one daughter and one son

4. _____ lives in Colorado Springs.
   a. Elizabeth
   b. Diane
   c. Caroline

5. _____ are Elizabeth's grandchildren.
   a. Bill and Cliff
   b. Jessica and Cliff
   c. Diane and Caroline

6. Elizabeth drives back to work on _____.
   a. Saturday
   b. Sunday
   c. Monday

7. Diane and Mark live in _____.
   a. Iowa
   b. Colorado
   c. Denver

Supplemental Reading 5

This is a story about a student. It is a story about Elizabeth Carr, too. The student has some problems, and Elizabeth helps him. Read the story. When you read, try to find the answers to these questions:

1. Who is the student?
2. What are his problems?
3. Who helps him find an apartment?
4. Is the end of the story happy or sad?

Mike Gets an Apartment

Mike is a student. He is a foreign student at an English language school. He is a new student from Venezuela, and he wants to learn English quickly. He is living with his friends now. They have a small apartment near the school, but there is a problem. Mike likes to study. He wants to learn English, and he studies every night. His roommates don't like to study. They like to play music on their stereo. They like to play the piano and sing songs. They have parties every night, so Mike can't study. His roommates are not quiet. They are noisy. Mike wants a new apartment. One day he tells his roommates, "I am moving. I cannot live here with you. You are too noisy. I can't study. Good-bye."

Mike's roommates don't like to study.

Mike thinks it is easy to find a new apartment. He goes to school. He tells Elizabeth about his problem. He needs a new apartment today.

Mike goes to class. He feels hot. He has a fever, and his head hurts. He has a headache. He doesn't feel well. At lunch time he goes to the nurse. He has small, red spots on his arms and face. He has the chicken pox. Mike is sick, and he must go home. Mike is sad because he has no home. He wants a quiet place. He wants to sleep. He wants a new apartment. He does not want to go back to his old apartment. He says to Elizabeth, "Please help me find an apartment."

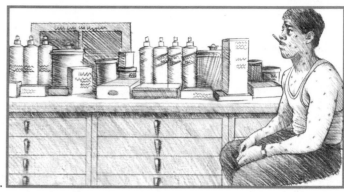

Mike is not feeling well.

Elizabeth takes Mike to a motel. Maybe he can stay there a few days. He can stay in a motel room while he is sick. It is quiet there. But the manager of the motel is looking at Mike. He is looking at the red spots. "He is sick," says the manager. "He can't stay at my motel. This is not a hospital. People will not stay here. This is bad for business. I am sorry, but he can't stay here."

Elizabeth and Mike are sad. Mike feels tired, and he wants to sleep. They go back to Elizabeth's car. The car is full. Mike's suitcases are in the car. Mike's clothes are in the car. Mike's books are in the car. All of Mike's things are in the car. But he has no place to go.

Elizabeth telephones two students. They are from Venezuela, too. They live in a small apartment near the school. Their names are Gloria and Maria. They are very nice. They are sorry for Mike. However, there is no room in their apartment. They only have one room. Mike cannot stay with them, so Elizabeth and Mike go back to school. What can they do?

Later, Gloria sees the manager of her apartment. He is a nice man. Gloria and Maria tell him about Mike. There is an empty apartment in the building. It is a small, one-room apartment with furniture. He can rent it to Mike today.

Gloria calls the school. Elizabeth answers the telephone and listens to Gloria's news. She is happy. Elizabeth tells Mike. Mike is happy. He has a new apartment. He has a place to sleep.

Elizabeth drives Mike to the new apartment. The manager meets Mike and rents the apartment to him. Gloria and Maria help Mike. They take the things from Elizabeth's car to Mike's apartment. Then they cook some soup for Mike, and he goes to sleep.

In a few days, Mike is better. He is not sick. He can go back to school. He is happy. He has a nice apartment. It is quiet, and he can study. He has two new friends, and they are nice. Mike has no more problems.

Mike is happy
in his new apartment.

CHECK YOUR UNDERSTANDING

Write T if the sentence is true (right) and F if the sentence is false (wrong). When the sentence is false, rewrite it with the correct information.

_____ 1. Mike is a teacher at a language school.

_____

_____ 2. Mike likes to study.

_____

_____ 3. Mike wants to move.

_____

_____ 4. Elizabeth has the chicken pox.

_____

_____ 5. Mike stays at the motel.

_____

_____ 6. Elizabeth talks to two students from Mexico.

_____

_____ 7. Mike goes back to his old apartment.

_____

_____ 8. Mike finds an apartment.

_____

Exercise 2

Circle the letter of the best answer.

1. Mike is from _____.
    a. America
    b. Venezuela
    c. Mexico

2. Mike can't study because _____.
    a. he doesn't speak English
    b. his roommates are too quiet
    c. his roommates are too noisy

3. _____ helps Mike find an apartment.
    a. Elizabeth
    b. His roommate
    c. The motel manager

4. Gloria and Maria are _____.
    a. teachers
    b. apartment managers
    c. students

5. At the end of the story, Mike lives _____.
    a. with his roommates
    b. alone in an apartment
    c. with Elizabeth

Supplemental Reading 6

Tom and Mike Carr like adventures, but adventures are expensive. What jobs do Tom and Mike have? How can they get the money for their adventure trips? How can they get the vacation time for their trips? The reading below will give you some answers to these questions.

Doing What You Want

Tom and Mike Carr like climbing mountains. They like ice climbing, skiing, mountain biking, and other exciting sports. But these sports all need equipment, and the equipment is expensive. They also like to travel to foreign countries, and these trips are expensive. It isn't easy to get the time and money to go on adventures, but they find ways to get these things. They find ways to do what they want to do.

For example, Tom and Mike are very good at sports. They are excellent skiers. One day, a ski company asks Tom to test some of their new equipment. They give him ski equipment and clothes to test. Tom doesn't have to pay for these things. This saves him money. Because Tom and Mike are twins, they can both use the clothes and equipment. This is another way they can save money. But how do they find the time?

Tom and Mike each have jobs, but the jobs are not their careers. They put up walls in new buildings. Tom and Mike work together all day. It is a hard job, but the pay is good.

Sometimes they get tired of working together. It isn't easy working with a brother, but they have a reason for working. Their goal is to save money for an adventure. When they save enough money, Tom and Mike leave their jobs. They will find new jobs when they come back.

The future may have different jobs and different goals, but it will also have adventures. Tom majored in premedical studies in college. He thinks he might study sports medicine in graduate school. Mike majored in geology. He is studying environmental science in graduate school. They want to continue having fun, going on adventures, and learning.

CHECK YOUR UNDERSTANDING

Answer the questions with the correct information.

1. Name three sports Tom and Mike like.

_____

_____

_____

2. Name two things that Tom and Mike need to have for their adventures.

_____

_____

3. How does the ski company help Tom and Mike?

   _____

4. Why is their job (putting up walls) a good one for Tom and Mike?

   _____

5. What will Tom and Mike do in the future?

   _____

Supplemental Reading 7

Mike and Tom Carr climbed a high mountain in Peru. They also climb mountains in North America. How high are the mountains of North America? Are they higher or lower than Chacraraju in Peru? Study the chart below.

HIGH MOUNTAINS OF NORTH AMERICA				
Name of Mountain	Group of Mountains	Country or State	Height (in feet)	Height (in meters)
Mount McKinley	Alaska Range	Alaska, USA	20,320	6,194
Mount Logan	St. Elias Mountains	Canada	19,850	6,050
Citlaltepetl	New Volcano Range	Mexico	18,700	5,700
Mount Whitney	Sierra Nevada	California, USA	14,494	4,418
Mount Elbert	Rocky Mountains	Colorado, USA	14,433	4,399

CHECK YOUR UNDERSTANDING

Read the sentences below. Fill in the blanks with information from the chart above.

High Mountains of North America

The highest mountains in North America are in a group of mountains in Alaska and Canada. This group of mountains is _____. The highest mountain in this group is Mount McKinley in Alaska. _____ is 20,320 feet (_____ meters) high. The Alaska Range goes from Alaska into Canada. The second highest mountain in North America is part of the Alaska Range in _____. Mount Logan is the name of the mountain. It is _____ feet (6,050 meters) high.

147

Mexico has another group of North America's highest mountains. These mountains are _____, or mountains that have fire and smoke. There are three very high volcanoes in Mexico. The highest of this group is _____. It is 18,700 feet (5,700 meters) high.

_____ is in the Sierra Nevada, a group of mountains in California. It is 14,494 feet (4,418 meters) high. It is the second highest mountain in the United States.

The Rocky Mountains are a large group of high mountains in North America. The Rocky Mountains go from Canada through the United States to Mexico. The highest mountain in this group is Mount Elbert in the state of _____. Mount Elbert is _____ feet (4,399 meters) high.

In Chapter 4, you read about the *Julia Belle Swain* and Captain Dennis Trone. Did you think about the people who take the trip? Why do people like to travel on the *Julia Belle Swain*? Do you want to take the trip? In the following reading, you can read about why people like to travel on the *Julia Belle Swain*.

A Journey Back in Time

The *Julia Belle Swain* travels on the Mississippi River from Le Claire, Iowa, to Galena, Illinois. The people ride the boat to Galena and back to Le Claire. The trip lasts two days. Why do people take this trip? The boat doesn't go to large cities. It doesn't take them to visit friends and family. It doesn't take them to work. The boat trip takes a long time. In their cars, people can travel to Galena in just two hours.

However, thousands of people take this trip each year. Most of the people on the boat are from Illinois, Iowa, or other nearby states. Some tourists come from the east coast or the west coast. Sometimes a foreign visitor rides the *Julia Belle Swain*.

People go on the *Julia Belle Swain* for many reasons. Many people want to see the Mississippi River, the most famous river in the United States. It is a good way to see the river. The boat is very slow. It travels only 12 miles per hour. The passengers can easily watch the banks of the river go by. In cars on a highway, travelers go fast. They usually drive 55 miles per hour. At that speed, it is not easy to watch the river.

One man explains his reasons in this way: "I can get away from my business and the telephone. I can relax. And the food is delicious."

The passengers can relax on the *Julia Belle Swain*.

A woman says, "I love the sounds of the boat. Because of the steam engine, the boat sounds like a living, breathing animal, not a machine. The paddlewheel hitting the water sounds like the heartbeat of the boat."

The boat takes another woman on a very unusual trip. "For me," she says, "a trip on the *Julia Belle Swain* is a journey back in time to days when traveling was slow. Life and boats moved more slowly then. I can imagine that the calendar has turned back 100 years. I see the world as my great-grandparents saw it."

The *Julia Belle Swain* takes people away from the fast, modern world. They can relax, enjoy the view, and think of past times. Because of the *Julia Belle Swain,* they can relive a little bit of history. That is a very special kind of trip.

CHECK YOUR UNDERSTANDING

Exercise 1

Write T if the sentence is true (right) and F if the sentence is false (wrong). When the sentence is false, rewrite it with the correct information.

_____   1.   The *Julia Belle Swain* takes people to large cities.

_____

_____   2.   Many people take the trip on the *Julia Belle Swain* because it is very fast.

_____

_____   3.   Most of the people who take the trip on the *Julia Belle Swain* come from nearby states.

_____

Exercise 2

Circle the letter of the best answer.

1.   The man in paragraph 4 likes to take the trip because _____.
   a.   he is a businessman
   b.   the boat has a telephone for him to use
   c.   he can relax

2.   The woman in paragraph 5 thinks the boat _____.
   a.   sounds like a living animal
   b.   has a very noisy paddlewheel
   c.   is an old machine

3.   The woman in paragraph 6 likes the trip because _____.
   a.   the trip is slow
   b.   she goes with her great-grandparents
   c.   she feels like she is living in the past

Exercise 3

Write answers to the following questions.

1. In paragraph 7, the writer tells again the main reasons for taking a trip on the *Julia Belle Swain*. What are the three reasons?

   _____

   _____

   _____

2. What is the best reason to take the trip **in your opinion**?

   _____

Supplemental Reading 9

The Mississippi River is a very big river. It is a very important river, too. This reading is about the size and importance of the Mississippi River.

The Big Water

The Mississippi River gets its name from American Indians. The Algonquin Indians called the river *Misi Sipi,* which means "big water." Other Indians called it "The Father of Rivers." The Indian names tell us about the size and importance of this North American river.

The Mississippi River is the longest river in North America. It runs south from the state of Minnesota, forming the borders of nine states, before it flows through the city of New Orleans to the Gulf of Mexico. It is 2,348 miles (3,779 kilometers) long. Two other very large rivers, the Missouri River and the Ohio River, flow into the Mississippi. These rivers carry the water from 1,244,000 square miles (3,221,000 square kilometers) of land to the sea. The river is also wide. At many places the distance from one side to the other is one and a half miles (more than two kilometers).

This big river is important, too. In the past, Indians used the river for transportation and food. They traveled up and down the river in canoes. They ate the river's fish. The first Europeans in the New World—the Spanish and the French—used the great river to explore the lands of North America. In the 1880s the river became important for transporting people, cotton, and food.

In the 1800s people built railroads. When the railroads came, the river was not as important for transportation of people. However, today boats called barges still carry many things up and down the river. They carry grain, iron, and coal to important cities along the river. Some barges are 1,500 feet (457 meters) long.

The big river is an important part of America's present and past.

CHECK YOUR UNDERSTANDING

Circle the letter of the best answer.

1. The reading is about _____.
   a. the Mississippi River
   b. the size of the Mississippi River
   c. the size and importance of the Mississippi River
   d. the American Indians

2. The name "Mississippi" comes from _____.
   a. Spanish
   b. French
   c. an Indian language
   d. English

3. _____ flow into the Mississippi River.
   a. The Gulf of Mexico
   b. The Missouri and Ohio rivers
   c. The Algonquin Indians
   d. The longest river in North America

4. Paragraph 2 has many facts about the Mississippi River. These facts tell the reader that _____.
   a. the Mississippi River is long and wide
   b. the Mississippi River is important for transportation
   c. the Mississippi River was important to American Indians

5. The first Europeans to use the Mississippi River were _____.
   a. the Spanish and the French
   b. the Indians
   c. the Americans
   d. the English

6. The Indians used the river _____.
   a. to make a railroad
   b. to travel and get food
   c. to make canoes

7. When the railroads came, the river was *not* so important for _____.
   a. traveling
   b. fishing
   c. carrying grain, iron, and coal

Supplemental Reading 10

The American farm family in Chapter 5 has lived in the same area for more than 100 years. However, many American families are different. Many families move. This reading is about Americans who move. When you read, find the answers to these questions: Why do people move? Is moving good or bad for people?

Americans on the Move

Every year millions of Americans move. In 1987, 39.4 million Americans moved. That is 17 percent of the people in the United States. Some of the people moved from one house to another house in the same city. But many Americans moved to other cities and states.

People move for many reasons. Some move because they want to find better jobs. Young people move to go to college. Sometimes a company asks people to move to another city to start a new company. Some people want to leave their pasts behind them and start new lives. Other people move because they want adventure.

Since the beginning of their country, Americans have been "on the move." In the 1600s and 1700s, the people who started the United States moved here from other countries. In the 1800s, Americans moved from the eastern states to the west. These people moved because they wanted a better life. Today, many Americans still think that they can move to a better life.

Sometimes moving is good for people, but sometimes it is very hard. Many times people get better jobs and make more money. They also make more friends. They can see new places and learn new things. However, moving can be difficult, too. Moving sometimes causes problems for families. When they move to a new place, there may be no one to help them with their problems. Children do not see their grandparents, aunts, and uncles. They have to leave their friends and go to different schools. Sometimes people who move are very lonely.

Moving is sometimes good and sometimes bad for people. It has advantages and disadvantages. However, millions of Americans choose to move every year. The advantages are more important to them. Moving is an important part of the past and present of the United States.

CHECK YOUR UNDERSTANDING

Exercise 1

Write T if the sentence is true (right) and F if the sentence is false (wrong). When the sentence is false, rewrite it with the correct information.

_____ 1. In 1987, 39.4 million Americans moved to another country.

_____

_____ 2. In the past, Americans did not move often.

_____

_____ 3. Moving sometimes makes problems for families.

_____

_____ 4. Some people move because they want to start new lives.

_____

_____ 5. People who move are sometimes lonely.

_____

_____ 6. Moving is very bad for people.

_____

Exercise 2

Answer the questions with short answers.

1. Why do people move? List the reasons here.

_____

_____

_____

2. What are the advantages (good things) about moving?

_____

_____

_____

3. What are the disadvantages (bad things) about moving?

_____

_____

_____

Supplemental Reading 11

In a business, the owners keep a record of expenses and income. Expenses are all the money they pay. Income is all the money they get. When income is more than expenses, the business owners make a profit. Profit is the money that business owners can use for their families, homes, food, travel, and all personal expenses.

Farmers are business owners. They must make a profit. They need the money for their family expenses. In "Raising Sheep," you can read more about the Graber family. What work must they do to raise sheep? Can they make a profit? What things help them to make a profit?

Raising Sheep

It is January in Illinois. Many farmers can relax in the winter months. The harvest is over, and the farmers have sold their corn and soybeans. It is three months before spring planting. Some farmers take a vacation trip to Florida, where the weather is warm. However, the Graber family has sheep. Late January is a very busy time for sheep farmers.

In the months of January, February, and March, the sheep are having baby sheep, or lambs. The Grabers plan that the sheep will have their lambs at this time of year. This is a good time because the Grabers have no work with the corn and soybeans.

When the sheep are having lambs, Cecil Graber must check the sheep often. Cecil must be near because the sheep sometimes have problems with the birth of their lambs. He has to stay up late and get up in the middle of the night and very early in the morning to go to the sheep barn. "We work all the time during these months," says his wife, Susan. "We have to stay home. There is no time for visiting or traveling."

Cecil puts the sheep into lambing pens before they have the lambs. When the lambs are born, Cecil moves the mothers and babies to other pens. When a sheep has twins, he puts her and her lambs into the twin pen. The sheep that have only one lamb are in a different pen. The mother sheep with twins gets more food because she must have milk for two lambs. "We don't want to give so much food to a mother who is feeding only one lamb," explains Susan. "When we feed her the same as we feed the mother of twins, she just gets too fat."

Raising sheep is a lot of hard work, but Cecil Graber enjoys it.

156

Large sheep farms have automated feeding systems. Machines weigh and move the feed to the animals. Machines bring water to the animals, and machines clean out the pens. The Grabers do not have machines for this work. They do all of this work by hand. It is heavy, dirty work.

In the early summer, the Grabers take the lambs to market. They sell the lambs, which weigh 100–200 pounds, for meat. In the past year, the Grabers sold 250 lambs. They also sell sheep that have only one lamb. In this way, they get sheep that have more lambs. In the past eight years, the Graber family has improved its lamb production from 1.2 lambs for each female sheep to 1.75 lambs for each female.

In addition to meat, the sheep produce wool. The Grabers have white and black sheep. The white sheep are kept mainly for meat. The black sheep are raised mainly for wool.

A sheep shearer comes to the farm in December and June to shear, or cut the wool from, the sheep. He shears the white sheep in December only. In this way, the farmers can be sure that the sheep will stay in the barn during the winter. In the barn they can have their lambs in warmth and safety. When the sheep have their warm wool coats, they leave the barn, and they might have their lambs in the snow. The shearer cuts the wool from the black sheep in December and June. The black sheep are wool producers. Their wool grows longer and faster than the wool of the white sheep.

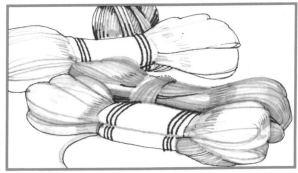

The factory makes the wool into yarn and sends it back to Susan.

The Grabers send their wool to a factory. The factory makes the wool into yarn and sends the yarn back to Susan. Then Susan must sell the yarn back to shops. The Graber farm can make a profit on the wool in this way. Many farmers sell the wool, not the yarn. However, the price of the wool is low. Farmers can pay only for the shearing with this money. They cannot make a profit.

Many Illinois farmers stopped raising animals because they did not make a profit. Raising corn and soybeans made more profit. The Grabers did not stop raising sheep. They raised sheep, corn, and soybeans. In the past, there were some difficult years when the sheep brought no profit. Now, they are happy that they have sheep. The price of lambs is high. Now, raising sheep is good business.

CHECK YOUR UNDERSTANDING

Answer the questions with the correct information.

1. When do sheep farmers work very hard? Why is this time very busy?

   _____

2. A sheep that has twins is in a twin pen. A sheep that has one lamb is in another pen. Why does Cecil Graber do this?

   _____

3. The Graber sheep have 1.75 lambs for each female sheep. When 100 female sheep have lambs, how many lambs do the Grabers have?

   _____

4. Why are the black sheep important?

   _____

5. Who cuts the wool from the sheep?

   _____

6. Why do they shear the white sheep in December?

   _____

7. Why can they shear the black sheep two times in one year?

   _____

8. The Grabers make a profit on the wool from their sheep. Other sheep farmers do not. Why can the Grabers make a profit on their wool?

   _____

9. Why did many Illinois farmers stop raising sheep?

   _____

10. Why is raising sheep good business now?

   _____

Supplemental Reading 12

Elizabeth Brier was Julia Brier's sister-in-law. She was married to William Brier. In 1850, she and her husband went west. They did not go across the United States. They did not follow the trail of Julia Brier and her family. This is a letter to Julia. It tells about Elizabeth's trip west.

A Letter to Julia

September 7, 1850
San Francisco

Dear Julia,

It is so nice to be in California. We arrived two days ago. We asked a lot of questions, and now we know you are living in Santa Cruz. We want you to visit us as soon as possible. I will tell you a little about our trip, but you must come to San Francisco to hear the details.

Our trip west began in late February. I think you and your family were already in California. We waited to hear from you before we left, but no letter arrived in time. We left without knowing about your trip. I thought about you many times during our trip. I am sure your trip was easier, and I thought, "What a pity, we did not follow Julia."

We left our home in Crawfordsville, Indiana, for Indianapolis by sleigh. It was winter, and this was the easiest way to move across the snow. From Indianapolis we took a train to Madison, Indiana. It cost $2.50 each. Then we took a riverboat on the Ohio River. The boat took us to Cincinnati, Ohio, and then to Pittsburgh, Pennsylvania. Our boat journey ended in Brownsville, Pennsylvania.

We did not stay long in Brownsville. Our next form of transportation was a stagecoach. We rode 73 miles to Cumberland, Maryland, and took another train to Baltimore and finally to Washington, D.C.

When we got to Washington, there were no ships. We went to New York because we wanted to get a ship from there, but we had to wait a month. Finally we left New York on board the SS *Panama*.

We reached the Atlantic side of the county of Panama in May, but we still had to cross Panama to get to the Pacific Ocean. That journey across Panama was very hard. We rode mules over steep, mountain trails. It was a long, six-day journey through the jungle. I had nightmares about the journey many times. I will never forget the spiders, snakes, monkeys, and other fearful things I saw along the trail. I'm sure your trip was easier. I know you passed through a desert. I prefer desert to the jungle.

On June 6, 1850, we reached Panama City. There were more than 3,000 Americans waiting for transportation by sea to California. We had to wait for a ship. During the wait, I became very sick. We moved to an island off the coast of Panama. I recovered soon on the island, and at the end of August we left the island for California. We arrived just two days ago. Please come to San Francisco to see us. We want to hear about your trip to California. Was your trip long, too? We are staying at the Parker House. I look forward to your visit.

Your loving sister-in-law,

Elizabeth Naylor Brier

CHECK YOUR UNDERSTANDING

Exercise 1

Elizabeth and her husband used many kinds of transportation during their trip. Here are some pictures of the many ways they traveled.

a

b

c

d

e

Look back at the reading and find out what kind of transportation they used between these places. Write the letter of the picture that matches the kind of transportation and the name of this kind of transportation in the blanks.

Where?	Picture	Name
1. Crawfordsville to Indianapolis	_____	_____
2. Indianapolis to Madison	_____	_____
3. Madison to Brownsville	_____	_____
4. Brownsville to Cumberland	_____	_____
5. New York to Panama	_____	_____

Exercise 2

Answer the questions with the correct information.

1. Why did they go to New York?

_____

2. How did Elizabeth and her husband cross the country of Panama from the Atlantic side to the Pacific side?

_____

3. How many months did it take Elizabeth to get to California?

_____

4. Why does Elizabeth think Julia's trip was easier?

_____

5. Was Julia's trip easier? Why or why not?

_____

_____

Julia Brier walked across a hot, dry valley of salt during her trip to California. The name of this place is Death Valley. This reading has many facts about this place.

Death Valley

Death Valley is in California. It is a large, wide valley about 130 miles (210 kilometers) long and 6–14 miles (9–22 kilometers) wide. The floor of the valley is mostly salt.

Death Valley is the lowest point in the United States. There are many high mountains around Death Valley, but the valley is actually 282 feet (85 meters) below sea level. Mount Whitney, the highest point in California, is 75 miles away. Mount Whitney is 14,494 feet (14,418 meters) above sea level.

Death Valley is also the hottest and driest place in the United States. Sometimes the temperature is 134° Fahrenheit (56° Celsius). However, sometimes in the winter the temperature is 15°F (-9.4°C).

This valley has very little water in it. It rains about two inches in one year. Some years there is no rain. There are not many plants in the valley, but there are some small desert plants.

In 1849 a group of settlers and gold seekers crossed this valley. This group named the place Death Valley because many people in the group died during the trip.

Today many tourists visit Death Valley, but they usually do not go there during the summer months.

CHECK YOUR UNDERSTANDING

Answer the questions with the correct information.

1. How wide and long is Death Valley?

   _____

2. What is the temperature range in Death Valley?

   _____

3. How many feet below sea level is Death Valley?

   _____

4. How many feet above sea level is the top of Mount Whitney?

   _____

Supplemental Reading 14

In 1849 Julia Brier left Illinois to move to California. Many people moved to California during this time. This reading tells us why.

The California Gold Rush

The year 1848 was an important year for California. First, it became part of the United States. Second, someone found gold there. The discovery of gold changed California's history.

In the early 1840s, California was not a state in the United States. The Mexican government controlled the area, but many people were moving to California from the United States. These American settlers and the United States government wanted California to be a state. There was a war between the United States and Mexico from 1846 to 1848. The two governments made an agreement in 1848, and the Mexican government gave up control of California. On February 2, 1848, California became a part of the United States. However, it was a territory, not a state.

On January 24, 1848, James W. Marshall made an important discovery. He was working for John A. Sutter, who was building a sawmill. A sawmill is a place to cut wood for houses. This sawmill was on the American River. On this famous day, Mr. Marshall saw something yellow in the river near the sawmill. He reached into the water and took out some small pieces of metal. They were gold! The gold was coming from the hills and going into the river.

Many people came to California to find gold and to be rich.

Soon people in the east heard the news: There was gold in the rivers of California! They began to dream of gold. They came to California to find gold. They wanted to be rich.

The way to California was not easy. People had to travel by covered wagon. It was a long, difficult journey. Many people died. "The Forty-Niners" was a nickname for the people who came to California to look for gold in 1849. In 1848 there were only about 14,000 American settlers in California. After the gold rush started, about 100,000 new settlers came to California. The population of the area grew quickly, and California became the 31st state on September 9, 1850.

Californians remember this part of their history today. The gold rush was an exciting event in American history. Other states also had rushes for gold and silver, but the California gold rush in 1849 was the most famous.

CHECK YOUR UNDERSTANDING

Exercise 1

Answer the questions with short answers.

1. What country controlled the area of California in 1846?

    _____

2. When did California become part of the United States?

    _____

3. What important event happened on January 24, 1848?

    _____

4. Where did this happen?

    _____

5. When did California become a state?

    _____

Exercise 2

Look at the chart below. Choose one state and answer the questions with short answers.

1. What is the name of the state?

    _____

2. What is the state capital?

    _____

3. In what year did it become a state?

    _____

4. California is the 31st state. What rank does your state have?

    _____

5. What state is the first state?

    _____

6. What state is the newest state?

    _____

THE UNITED STATES OF AMERICA			
State Name	**Entered Union**	**Rank**	**Capital**
Alabama	December 14, 1819	22	Montgomery
Alaska	January 3, 1959	49	Juneau
Arizona	February 14, 1912	48	Phoenix
Arkansas	June 15, 1836	25	Little Rock
California	September 9, 1850	31	Sacramento
Colorado	August 1, 1876	38	Denver
Connecticut	January 9, 1788	5	Hartford
Delaware	December 7, 1787	1	Dover
Florida	March 3, 1845	27	Tallahassee
Georgia	January 2, 1788	4	Atlanta

State Name	Entered Union	Rank	Capital
Hawaii	August 21, 1959	50	Honolulu
Idaho	July 3, 1890	43	Boise
Illinois	December 3, 1818	21	Springfield
Indiana	December 11, 1816	19	Indianapolis
Iowa	December 28, 1846	29	Des Moines
Kansas	January 29, 1861	34	Topeka
Kentucky	June 1, 1792	15	Frankfort
Louisiana	April 30, 1812	18	Baton Rouge
Maine	March 15, 1820	23	Augusta
Maryland	April 28, 1788	7	Annapolis
Massachusetts	February 6, 1788	6	Boston
Michigan	January 26, 1837	26	Lansing
Minnesota	May 11, 1858	32	St. Paul
Mississippi	December 10, 1817	20	Jackson
Missouri	August 10, 1821	24	Jefferson City
Montana	November 8, 1889	41	Helena
Nebraska	March 1, 1867	37	Lincoln
Nevada	October 31, 1864	36	Carson City
New Hampshire	June 21, 1788	9	Concord
New Jersey	December 18, 1787	3	Trenton
New Mexico	January 6, 1912	47	Santa Fe
New York	July 26, 1788	11	Albany
North Carolina	November 21, 1789	12	Raleigh
North Dakota	November 2, 1889	39	Bismarck
Ohio	March 1, 1803	17	Columbus
Oklahoma	November 16, 1907	46	Oklahoma City
Oregon	February 14, 1859	33	Salem
Pennsylvania	December 12, 1787	2	Harrisburg
Rhode Island	May 29, 1790	13	Providence
South Carolina	May 23, 1788	8	Columbia
South Dakota	November 2, 1889	40	Pierre
Tennessee	June 1, 1796	16	Nashville
Texas	December 29, 1845	28	Austin
Utah	January 4, 1896	45	Salt Lake City
Vermont	March 4, 1791	14	Montpelier
Virginia	June 25, 1788	10	Richmond
Washington	November 11, 1889	42	Olympia
West Virginia	June 20, 1863	35	Charleston
Wisconsin	May 29, 1848	30	Madison
Wyoming	July 10, 1890	44	Cheyenne

Supplemental Reading 15

Julia Brier celebrated two holidays during her trip from Illinois to California. She celebrated Thanksgiving Day and Christmas. People in many parts of the world celebrate Christmas, but Thanksgiving Day is an American holiday. Thanksgiving Day is important in Chapter 7. As you read, find the answers to these questions: Who started Thanksgiving Day? Why did they celebrate? How do Americans celebrate Thanksgiving Day today?

The Story of Thanksgiving Day

Many American holidays are from Europe because many of the people who settled in North America came from there. They brought their holidays with them to the New World. Thanksgiving Day, however, is a truly American holiday. It started in America. The first Thanksgiving Day was in 1621 in what is now Massachusetts. The people who celebrated the first Thanksgiving were the Pilgrims.

The Pilgrims were a group of people from England. They sailed to America on a boat named the *Mayflower*. They left England because of religious reasons. In England they could not follow their religion in the way that they wanted. They wanted to settle in a new land.

The Pilgrims arrived in the New World in the winter of 1620. Soon after the settlers arrived, Squanto, an Indian, came to them. He showed them how to build houses for the winter. But the first months were very difficult because the winter was very cold. The settlers did not have much food. Nearly half of them died in that first winter.

Then in the spring, Squanto showed the settlers how to plant corn, an American grain. He showed them how to catch the fish in the streams. The settlers also planted European grains and peas that they had brought with them. In the summer and fall the settlers had plenty to eat. They were very thankful to God and to the Indian Squanto for his help. The Pilgrims had a feast to celebrate and to show their thanks. They invited Massoit, the chief of the Wapanoag Indians, who lived nearby. He brought 90 Indian men with him. The Pilgrims prepared corn, duck, goose, berries, and fish. The Indians brought deer meat. The celebration lasted for three days.

This celebration is now a tradition. Every year on the fourth Thursday of November, people in the United States celebrate Thanksgiving. On this day, families come together for a traditional dinner. This dinner usually consists of roast turkey, cranberry sauce, and vegetables. The vegetables are often corn, squash, or sweet potatoes. These are vegetables that the early American settlers grew in their first years in America. The Pilgrims hunted wild turkeys in the forests of New England and cranberries grew wild there, too. Dessert on Thanksgiving Day is usually pumpkin pie, made from another American plant.

This is a day for families. Parents, children, grandparents, aunts, and uncles celebrate together. Today, when Americans live far from their families, people often celebrate with friends. Families often invite friends who live alone to have dinner with them. It is a time for Americans to give thanks, to be with their families and friends, and to remember the early settlers of their country and the Indians who helped them.

CHECK YOUR UNDERSTANDING

Answer each question with the correct information.

1. Why is Thanksgiving a "truly American holiday"?

   _____

2. Who were the Pilgrims?

   _____

3. Why did they leave England?

   _____

4. Why was their first winter in the New World difficult?

   _____

5. How did Squanto help the settlers?

   _____

6. Why did the settlers have the feast?

    _____

7. Why did they invite the Indians?

    _____

8. When do Americans celebrate Thanksgiving Day?

    _____

9. Why do Americans eat traditional foods on Thanksgiving Day?

    _____

10. What are three reasons for celebrating Thanksgiving Day today?

    _____

Supplemental Reading 16

Barbecued ribs are a favorite meal of many Americans. To *barbecue* means to cook over an open fire, usually wood. Many Americans barbecue meat in the summer because they can cook outside. People usually put a sauce on the meat when it is cooking. Many people have a family recipe for barbecue sauce. Daddy Bruce got his recipe for barbecue sauce from his grandmother. Americans use barbecue sauce for many meats, but very often for ribs and chicken. Here is a recipe for barbecue sauce.

A Recipe for Barbecued Ribs

Barbecue Sauce Ingredients
  2 small onions
  1 clove of garlic
  1 12-oz. can of tomato paste
  2/3 c. of olive oil
  1/2 c. of wine vinegar
  1/4 c. of Worcestershire sauce
  1/4 c. brown sugar
  1 t. chili powder
  1 t. dry mustard
  1 T. Tabasco sauce (or to taste)
  4 lbs. ribs

  Chop the onions into very small pieces. Peel the garlic and crush it in a garlic press or with the back of a spoon. In a saucepan, mix the tomato paste, olive oil, vinegar, Worcestershire sauce, and brown sugar. Add onions, garlic, chili powder, dry mustard, and Tabasco. Add more Tabasco or chili powder for a spicier sauce. Bring to a boil over medium heat. Reduce heat to low and simmer for ten minutes.
  Cook the ribs over medium-hot coals until they are well done. When the ribs are almost ready to eat, brush them with the sauce. Cook the ribs for ten minutes more. Turn the meat once during this time. (Do not put the sauce on when you begin to cook the ribs. The sauce will burn before they are ready.)

Notes:
12-oz. can = the size of the can (This information is on the can.)
c. = cup
T. or tbsp. = tablespoon
t. or tsp. = teaspoon
to taste = put in the amount that tastes good to you
lbs. = pounds

CHECK YOUR UNDERSTANDING

Answer these questions about the recipe.

1. What must you do with the onions before you add them to the sauce?

    _____

2. How can you make the sauce spicier?

    _____

3. How long do you cook the sauce?

    _____

4. When do you put the sauce on the meat?

    _____

5. Why don't you put the sauce on the meat when you begin to cook it?

    _____

Supplemental Reading 17

In Chapter 8, you read about a storyteller. Joe Hayes tells folktales from New Mexico. Here is a traditional folktale. Many cultures have this story or one like it. Do you know a story like this from your culture? Which other chapter in *Ready to Read* do you think of when you read this story?

City Mouse and Country Mouse

One day Country Mouse worked very hard. It was fall, and winter was coming soon. He had to find corn and seeds for the winter. He found some fat, delicious, yellow corn that day and carried it to his storehouse. In the storehouse he kept food for the long winter months. He was tired after working hard, but he was very happy about the corn. "It will taste wonderful when the snow covers the ground," he thought. He sat down to his evening meal. Country Mouse was eating seeds, listening to the songs of the birds, and watching the sunset. Suddenly another mouse ran up to him.

"Hello, Cousin! I'm here to visit you," said the visitor.

"Hello, City Mouse!" answered Country Mouse. "I'm so happy to see you. Come into my home and eat some supper with me. Are you tired after your long trip?"

"Yes, I'm tired, but I'm so glad to see you. I have a lot to tell you about your city cousins," said City Mouse.

Country Mouse
got some of the fat,
yellow corn
for his city cousin.

Country Mouse got some of the fat, yellow corn for his city cousin. They ate together and talked and talked long into the night.

The next morning at breakfast Country Mouse said, "Yesterday I found some fat, yellow corn. Today I will carry more corn to my storehouse for the winter. You can come with me. You can take some corn to your storehouse in the city."

172

City Mouse laughed. "Ha, ha, ha! My storehouse! I don't need a storehouse in the city. There is so much food in the city. Look at me," she said, patting her fat stomach. "I eat a feast every day, in summer and winter. And I don't eat corn." City Mouse talked on and on about the delicious food in the city. Country Mouse began to think about cakes, cheese, and wine.

"Look at you," said City Mouse. "You are thin. Your life is hard. You work every day. And for what? For corn. Come to the city with me. You can stay for the winter. You will love it."

"We will eat a fine dinner," said City Mouse.

"I want to see this wonderful city," said Country Mouse. "I will come with you."

After breakfast, they packed some food for the long trip to the city. Country Mouse said good-bye to his friends. Then they left for the city.

The trip was long, but the cousins talked about the city on the way. Country Mouse was very excited. He walked faster and faster because he wanted to see the city.

When they came to the city, however, Country Mouse walked slowly. There was so much to see. "The city is very different from the country," said Country Mouse. The buildings were tall. There were cars and people everywhere. The noise hurt his ears. He did not see one cornfield. He could not hear the birds. It was evening, but he could not see the sun going down. He felt a little sad and a little afraid. But then he thought of the food and he walked fast again.

City Mouse took her cousin to her home in a tall apartment building. It was late in the evening. They were hungry after the long trip. On the dining room table was lots of food. "We will eat a fine dinner," said City Mouse proudly.

Country Mouse said, "Oh, the food is beautiful! It is wonderful, just as you told me!" He began to eat. First, he tried a dark chocolate cake. Then he tasted a bright red cherry on top of the cake. Next he found some cheese. Just when he was taking a drink of red wine from a tall glass, he heard a noise. He looked up. He saw two mean, green eyes looking at him. It was a cat!

"Run!" squeaked City Mouse. "Run for your life!"

Country Mouse ran. The cat's paw came down on his poor mouse tail, but he ran on. He saw a hole in the wall. He got inside just in time. His cousin City Mouse was there before him. They slept then because they were so tired, but Country Mouse did not sleep well. All night he heard the sound of the cat's breathing outside the hole.

The next morning at breakfast Country Mouse thanked his cousin. "Good-bye," he said.

"There are many wonderful things in the city, but I want to return to my own country home!"

City Mouse did not understand her cousin. She said, "Please stay longer."

But Country Mouse said, "No, thank you. I have so much work to do at home. I must get ready for the winter."

City Mouse said, "Good-bye! I will visit you soon, cousin," but at the same time she thought, "It's so far and I don't like the food. And what can I do in the country?"

Later that evening Country Mouse arrived at his country home. He had a supper of seeds. He listened to the birds and watched the sunset. That night he slept very well.

CHECK YOUR UNDERSTANDING

Exercise 1

The sentences below tell the important events in the story, "City Mouse and Country Mouse." However, the sentences are not in the right order. Put 1 by the first event, 2 by the second, and so on. The last event will have the number 10.

_____ The two cousins ate cake, cheese, and wine.

_____ City Mouse and Country Mouse traveled to the city together.

_____ The cousins ran away from a cat.

_____ Country Mouse could not sleep well.

_____ City Mouse came to visit her cousin Country Mouse.

_____ Country Mouse slept well.

_____ Country Mouse and City Mouse said good-bye.

_____ Country Mouse got some of the fat, yellow corn for his cousin.

_____ Country Mouse returned to his country home.

_____ City Mouse invited Country Mouse to come to the city.

Exercise 2

Many folktales teach lessons, or *morals.* What is the moral of this story?

_____

_____

Supplemental Reading 18

When Julia Brier was traveling to California, she and her family met some Sioux Indians. Her boys were very interested in the Sioux. This reading is about the Sioux.

The Story of the Sioux Indians of North America

There are many Indian tribes in North America. A tribe is a group of people. It is like a big family. One famous tribe is the Sioux Indian tribe. However, Sioux is not their name. They call themselves Dakota or Lakota. Where did the name Sioux come from? Who gave them this name?

The Dakota Indians lived in the area of North America west of the Great Lakes. This area is now Minnesota. The Dakota first met Europeans during the middle of the 17th century.

Another Indian tribe, the Chippewa, called the Dakota Indians "Na-dawe Su." This means "treacherous snakes" in their language. They used this name because the Sioux were their enemies. The French heard the name "Na-dawe Su" and called the Dakotas "Su." However, they wrote the word with a French spelling: Sioux. It was a misunderstanding by the French.

The Sioux did not use this name. They called themselves Dakota. The word "kota" means "friend," and "dakota" means "an alliance of friends." An alliance is a group of people. Because the Dakota tribe was very large, there were differences in the language. Some groups called themselves Dakota, and other groups called themselves Lakota.

In the beginning, when the Dakota Indians all lived in the area of Minnesota, there were seven tribes. As the Europeans moved west, the Dakota tribes moved further west, away from the Europeans. Four of the tribes formed the Santee, or Dakota Indians. Two of the tribes formed the Wiciyela, or the Nakota Indians, and the largest tribe formed the Teton, or Lakota Indians.

The Lakota Indians continued to move west, and by 1750 they were living in the area that is now North and South Dakota. The Lakota tribe was very big. It had smaller groups, or subtribes, within the main tribe. The Hunkpapa was one subtribe. The Lakota always camped in the shape of a circle. The Hunkpapa group always camped on the outside of the circle. It was their job to protect the inside of the circle. They were the real fighters. The word "hunkpapa" means "on the outside" in the Lakota language.

The wars with the Indians became very bad as the United States grew. The Indians fought many battles with the soldiers of the United States. One very famous Hunkpapa Lakota Indian was Sitting Bull. In 1876, there was a famous battle, the Battle of the Little Big Horn. Sitting Bull was one of the Indian leaders at the Battle of the Little Big Horn. George Custer was a general in the U.S. Army, and he was an Indian fighter. The Indians killed Custer and his soldiers in this battle. Sitting Bull and some of his followers ran away to Canada, but they returned to Standing Rock Reservation in 1881. In 1890, Sitting Bull was killed. He is buried in Mobridge, South Dakota.

Today most people call the Indians of this tribe Sioux, but their real name is Dakota or Lakota. There are about 68,000 Dakota Indians living in the United States today. They live on Indian reservations in North Dakota, South Dakota, Nebraska, and Montana.

CHECK YOUR UNDERSTANDING

Answer the questions with the correct information.

1. What does the word *dakota* mean?

   _____

2. What does the name *Na-dawe Su* mean?

   _____

3. Who gave the name *Sioux* to the Dakota Indians?

   _____

4. What is a tribe?

   _____

5. Why did the Dakota Indians move west?

   _____

6. What does *hunkpapa* mean?

   _____

7. What is a subtribe?

   _____

8. Who was General George Custer?

   _____

9. What happened to him at the Battle of the Little Big Horn?

   _____

10. Who was Sitting Bull and when did he die?

    _____

11. How many Dakota Indians live in the United States today?

    _____

You read about American Indians in Chapters 6, 8, and 9. The reading below tells you some facts about these people. It tells you some facts about the past and some facts about the present.

American Indians in the United States

Christopher Columbus came to the islands between North and South America in 1492. He thought that he was on an island east of India, so he called the people on the island Indians. We use the name American Indians for the people who first lived in North and South America. Another name for these people is Native Americans.

How many Indians lived in North America in 1492? No one knows exactly. There were probably between one and two million Indians at that time. They lived in all parts of North America. The largest groups lived on the west coast, the east coast, and in the area of Arizona and New Mexico. Some Indians lived in cities, and some lived in small villages. Others moved from place to place. Some hunted and fished. Others were farmers. The Indians were not all the same. There were many different Indian tribes, or groups of Indians. The tribes had different traditions, religions, and languages. In fact, there were more than 2,000 Indian languages.

In the 1600s, settlers came to North America from many parts of Europe. At first, the Indians and Europeans were friendly. There was so much land and only a few people. However, the Europeans, and later the Americans, took more and more land. The Indians in the east moved west. Many died in wars with the U.S. Army. In 1890, there were only about 248,000 Indians left in the United States.

After 1900 the number of Indians in the United States began to grow. In 1980 the U.S. government counted 1,534,000 Indians. About one-half of these Indians live in American cities. In 1987, 851,500 Indians lived on reservations.

Reservations are Indian-owned lands in the United States. When the U.S. government started Indian reservations in the 1800s, many Indians had to leave their land and move to reservations. There are about 250 Indian reservations. Thirty-one states in the United States have Indian reservations. The Indian reservations consist of about 54 million acres (218,535 square kilometers). The largest Indian reservation is the Navajo Reservation in the states of Arizona and New Mexico. It is 13,989,222 acres (56,613 square kilometers). Today, 131,379 Navajos live on this reservation.

In the 1800s, the Indians did not want to live on the reservations. Today, Indians are Americans who can live where they want. Many Indians live in American cities. However, many Indians want to live on their reservations now. In these places they can follow some of the Indian ways of their grandparents. Some speak the language of their tribe and follow the religion of their grandparents. On the reservation, they can pass on their culture and their land to their children.

CHECK YOUR UNDERSTANDING

Fill in the blanks in the following sentences about the reading, "American Indians in the United States."

    The name "Indians" comes from a mistake. _____ made this mistake because he thought that _____. Another name for American Indians is _____. In 1492, ____ million Indians lived in North America. American Indians lived in all parts of North America but the largest groups lived _____, _____, and _____. The word for groups of Indians is _____. These groups had different _____.

    The Indians moved west because _____. The number of Indians who lived in North America was only _____ in 1890. After _____ the Indian population began to grow.

    Today about _____ Indians live in the United States. About one-half of these Indians live _____ and one-half live _____. The Navajo Reservation in _____ and _____ is the largest Indian reservation in the United States.

Supplemental Reading 20

In Chapter 9, we read about Bonnie Jo Hunt. This story tells us more about her interest in music.

Bonnie Jo Starts to Sing

One day Bonnie Jo Hunt was listening to the radio in her home in Fort Yates, North Dakota. The music was very different. A symphony orchestra was playing on the radio.

"Oh, Father," she said, "What's that sound?"

"Oh, that's an orchestra," he said, and he told her about violins and flutes and trumpets.

After listening to the beautiful music, Bonnie Jo asked her father, "Will you please buy me an instrument?"

"No," her father said. "Too many parents buy their children instruments, and in two weeks the children don't want to play them."

Bonnie Jo's feelings were very hurt. Her father also said, "The piano is a good instrument for girls, but we move around too much. We can't have a piano. When we get a home, I will buy you a piano."

After four years Bonnie Jo still did not have a piano. She was ten years old, and one day she heard a voice singing on the radio. So again she asked her father, "What's that sound?"

"Oh, that's opera. You don't want to hear that. It's boring," her father said, and he turned off the radio. He also said, "All opera singers are big, fat people. You don't want to be an opera singer." But Bonnie Jo loved the sound of the singing voice, and she decided she wanted to be an opera singer. "I don't need an instrument if I sing," Bonnie Jo thought.

Bonnie Jo had a dream, but she was afraid to tell her family. She didn't want them to laugh at her. That summer her grandmother came to visit.

"Grandma will understand me," thought Bonnie Jo. So she walked over to her grandmother and said, "Grandma Robbins, do you know what I'm going to be when I grow up?"

"No, Bonnie Jo, what are you going to be?"

"I'm going to be an opera singer!"

Then her grandmother began to laugh and laugh. She had to sit down because she was laughing so hard. She couldn't talk.

"That is the most ridiculous thing I've ever heard," her grandmother said. "Don't you know opera singers need a loud voice? You don't have any volume. How can you sing?"

Bonnie Jo was mad at her grandmother because she had never heard Bonnie Jo sing. She decided at that moment, "I am going to get a strong voice and be an opera singer."

Bonnie Jo didn't tell anyone else her dream. She sang along with the radio. But nobody knew her dream. Then Bonnie Jo's family moved to Valier, Montana. It was a small town. Only 710 people lived there.

Bonnie Jo remembers a special morning when she was 12 years old. Her whole family was sitting at the breakfast table. Suddenly her mother said, "Bonnie Jo, I didn't know you could sing! Why didn't you tell me you could sing?" Bonnie Jo was surprised.

"I can't sing," she said.

"Yes, you can," her mother said. "Last night you were singing in your sleep, and you hit the most beautiful high notes. They were just like bells."

"Oh, no, I can't sing," Bonnie Jo said, but she was very happy.

This news was wonderful. Her mother knew she could sing. Bonnie Jo rushed out of the house to find her friend, Weasel.

When Bonnie Jo found Weasel, she said, "Let's enter that talent contest at the high school. We can sing." The contest was for high school students, and Bonnie Jo and Weasel were only in the seventh grade. However, not many people entered the contest, so they could be in it. They sang a song called "Sparkling Brown Eyes" and won the contest!

After this contest, people invited them to sing at concerts. Every year in Valier, there was a big concert. There was a lot of entertainment there, and the concert committee invited Bonnie Jo and Weasel to sing at this concert. But something terrible happened.

Their first song was "Yankee Doodle Dandy." They started to sing the song, and Weasel started to laugh. She could not stop laughing. She could not sing. Finally, she sat down on the stage and began to cry.

"I'm never going to sing again," Weasel cried.

"Oh, Weasel, don't be silly. Maybe the people think this is part of our act. Don't cry," said Bonnie Jo.

But Weasel kept on crying. "I'm so embarassed," she said. "Everyone hates me."

However, the people at the concert liked their singing. They invited Bonnie Jo and Weasel to sing at other places. But Weasel did not go, so Bonnie Jo begin to sing alone. She was a soloist at the age of 12.

CHECK YOUR UNDERSTANDING

Circle the letter of the best answer.

1. Bonnie Jo was _____ years old when she heard the orchestra on the radio.
   a. six
   b. ten
   c. twelve
   d. two

2. Bonnie Jo's father thought she should play a _____.
   a. piano
   b. violin
   c. flute
   d. guitar

3. Bonnie Jo's father didn't like the opera because _____.
   a. it was loud
   b. it was boring
   c. it was expensive
   d. it was on the radio

4. The first person Bonnie Jo told about her dream is her _____.
   a. father
   b. mother
   c. grandmother
   d. Weasel

5. Bonnie Jo's grandmother thought it was a silly idea because _____.
   a. Indians don't sing opera
   b. Bonnie Jo didn't have a loud voice
   c. she knew Bonnie Jo couldn't sing
   d. it costs a lot of money to study music

6. Bonnie Jo's mother first heard Bonnie Jo sing _____.
   a. in a concert in Valier
   b. with her friend Weasel
   c. in Fort Yates
   d. when Bonnie Jo was sleeping

7. Weasel could not finish the song because _____.
   a. she was angry
   b. she was laughing
   c. she didn't like singing
   d. everyone hated her

8. A soloist is _____.
   a. a young person who sings
   b. a person who sings with a friend
   c. a person who sings alone
   d. a person who doesn't sing

APPENDIX TWO

METRIC CONVERSIONS

People in the United States use a different standard of weights and measures. For example, if an American asks you "How tall are you?" they expect you to tell them your height in feet and inches, not in centimeters. Here are some useful conversions for you to use.

MILES × 1.609 = **KILOMETERS**
Hue's family traveled more than **600 miles** from Vietnam to Hong Kong.
600 miles × 1.609 = 965.4 kilometers
Tom and Mike walked **two miles** in two hours.
2 miles × 1.609 = 3.2 kilometers

FEET × 0.3048 = **METERS**
Mike and Tom fell **1,500 feet** down the mountain.
1,500 feet × .3048 = 457.2 meters

METERS × 3.28 = **FEET**
Chacraraju is **6,112 meters** high.
6,112 meters × 3.28 = 20,047 feet

ACRES ÷ 247.1 = **SQUARE KILOMETERS**
The farm is **550 acres,** which is 2.2 square kilometers.
550 acres ÷ 247.1 = 2.258 square kilometers

POUNDS × .454 = **KILOGRAMS**
Julia Brier weighed **75 pounds** after her journey.
75 pounds × .454 = 34.05 kilograms

KILOGRAMS × 2.2 = **POUNDS**
She weighed **45 kilograms** when she came to the United States.
45 kilograms × 2.2 = 99 pounds

FAHRENHEIT - 32/1.8 = **CELSIUS**
Sometimes the temperature in Death Valley is **134° Fahrenheit.**
134° Fahrenheit - 32/1.8 = 56.7° Celsius

(CELSIUS × 1.8) + 32 = **FAHRENHEIT**
Today it is **27° Celsius.**
(27° Celsius × 1.8) + 32 = 80.6° Fahrenheit